Dao De Jing
in Clear English

Including a Step-By-Step Translation

Dao De Jing in Clear English

Including a Step-By-Step Translation

by Laozi

Translation and Commentary by
Jeff Pepper and Xiao Hui Wang

IMAGIN8
PRESS

Copyright © 2018-2021 by Imagin8 Press LLC, all rights reserved.

Published in the United States by Imagin8 Press LLC, Verona, Pennsylvania, US. For information, contact us via email at info@imagin8press.com, or visit www.imagin8press.com.

Our books may be purchased directly in quantity at a reduced price, contact us at info@imagin8press.com for details.

Imagin8 Press, the Imagin8 logo and the sail image are all trademarks of Imagin8 Press LLC.

Cover and book design by Jeff Pepper
Artwork by Next Mars Media, Luoyang, China

Photo Credits:

- Page 292, Figure 1 (Laozi statue): Photo source: Thanato (own work) [CC BY-SA 3.0 (https://creativecommons.org/licenses/by-sa/3.0)], via Wikimedia Commons.

- Page 293 (Figure 2: Guodian slips): Original in Hubei Provincial Museum. Photo source: By Sharkman (own work) [CC BY-SA 3.0 (https://creativecommons.org/licenses/by-sa/3.0)], via Wikimedia Commons.

- Page 295 (Figure 3: Mawangdui silk texts): Original in Hunan Province Museum. Photo Source: https://en.wikipedia.org/wiki/Mawangdui_Silk_Texts, via Wikimedia Commons.

- Page 301 (Oracle bone script): Omniglot online encyclopedia of writing systems and languages (www.omniglot.com/chinese/jiaguwen.htm), Copyright © 1998-2018 Simon Ager, used by permission.

Typeset in Adobe Garamond (body), Senty Wen (Chinese calligraphy), Sim Sun and Calibri (step-by-step translations).

ISBN: 978-1952601361 (Hardcover edition)

Version 05a

ACKNOWLEDGEMENTS

We are deeply indebted to the many scholars who have labored to uncover, translate and interpret the Dao De Jing. We especially want to thank Dr. Bruce R. Linnell, whose *Minimalist Translation of the Dao De Jing by Lao Zi* (Gutenberg Project, 2015) was so helpful to us in this project. Translations that were particularly helpful were *Dao De Jing: The Book of the Way* (Moss Roberts, University of California Press, 2004), *Dao De Jing: A Philosophical Translation* (Roger Ames and David Hall, Ballantine Books, 2003), and the beautifully written and illustrated *Tao Te Ching* (Gia-Fu Feng and Jane English, Vintage Book, 1972). When we needed help with the original text, we often relied on the Chinese-language book 道德经 (Dao De Jing), annotated by Li Yan Wang (China Federation of Literary and Art Circles Publishing Corp, 2017). We are also grateful for the many online research tools listed in the Resources section at the end of this book.

Finally, we owe a debt of gratitude to William David Hetzel for his thorough review of the manuscript. And for their deep insights and thoughtful analysis of each chapter of the Dao De Jing, we can't say enough about the contributions from the members of the Dao Bums online discussion group www.thedaobums.com.

Of course, we take full responsibility for any and all errors. Please feel free to let us know if you find any, you can reach us at jeff@imagin8press.com.

Contents

Welcome   7

The Dao De Jing

    Dao Jing   13
    De Jing   143

Additional Information

    Translation Notes   293
    Glossary   306
    Resources   311
    About the Authors   313

Welcome

The eighty-one chapters of this book are like tasty morsels, set out carefully on a long buffet table. Candles are flickering. You have been invited to be an honored guest.

Come on in. Take a bite, chew it slowly. Try to taste all the flavors.

Later on, maybe take another bite or two.

No need to eat too much at once!

The Dao is the way of balance and harmony.

Dao De Jing

Part 1: Dao Jing

1

The Dao that can be spoken is not the eternal Dao.
The name that can be named is not the eternal name.
Nameless, the beginning of heaven and earth.
Named, the mother of ten thousand things.

Being empty, see the wonder.
Being present, see the appearance.
These two are the same but have different names,
This is mystery.

Mystery upon mystery,
The doorway to wonder.

The Dao that can be spoken is not the eternal Dao.

> 道可道非常道。
> Dào kě dào fēi cháng dào.

Path | can be | spoken | not | eternal/everlasting | path.

▶ This first line introduces us to the depth and mystery of Dao. As a noun, 道 (dào) literally means *path* or *road*, as a verb it's *to say*/*speak* and also *to tread/walk*. But it's also the way of nature, the natural flow of the universe, the mysterious force that is the mother of all things. In just six words, Laozi uses the poetic tension between the ordinary and extraordinary meanings of 道 to offer a glimpse into a deep wisdom.

▶ 非 (fēi): *not* or *against*.

▶ 常 (cháng) has several different meanings depending on context. Here it means *eternal or everlasting*. See the Glossary for more on the different meanings of 常 in the DDJ.

The name that can be named is not the eternal name.

> 名可名非常名。
> Míng kě míng fēi cháng míng.

Name | can be | named | not | eternal/everlasting | name.

▶ 名 (míng) is a common Chinese word meaning *name*. But at a deeper level, it is something's identity. If something is a nameless mystery, what happens when you try to give it a name?

Nameless, the beginning of heaven and earth.

> 无名，天地之始。
> Wú míng, tiān dì zhī shǐ.

No | name, | heaven | earth | of⇆ | beginning.

▶ 无 (wū): a deep negative, meaning *emptiness, absence, void*.

▶ 天 (tiān): *heaven/sky*, and 地 (dì): *earth/ground*, when combined, it means the entire universe.

▶ A note on grammar: 之 (zhī) is usually used as a possessive particle. It's like the English word *of*, but with the object before it and the subject after. So, "earth 之 beginning" means "beginning of earth." We use the symbol "of⇆" to indicate this in the word-by-word translation. However, if you see 之 at the end of a phrase or sentence it generally means "it," "them," or "this."

Named, the mother of ten thousand things.

> 有名，万物之母。
> Yǒu míng, wànwù zhī mǔ.

Has | name, | ten thousand things/creatures | of⇆ | mother.

▶ In modern Chinese 有名 (yǒumíng) means *famous*, but here it has the original meaning of *has name*, fitting nicely with 无名 (wúmíng), *nameless* in the previous line.

▶ 万物 (wàn wù): *ten thousand things*, everything in the material world.

Being empty, see the wonder.

> 故常无欲，以观其妙。
> Gù cháng wú yù, yǐ guān qí miào.

Therefore | often/usually | without | desire, | in order to | see | its | mystery.

▶ 妙 (miào): *mysterious, wonderful*.

▶ For brevity, we don't include 故常 (gù cháng), *therefore*, in the English translation of these two lines.

Being present, see the appearance.

> 常有欲，以观其徼。
> Cháng yǒu yù, yǐ guān qí jiào.

Often/usually | have | desire, | in order to | see | its | edges.

▶ 徼 (jiào): *boundary, border, edge.* Being engaged in this world can prevent us from seeing the still depths of the nameless mysteries.

These two are the same but have different names,
This is mystery.

> 此兩者同出而異名同，謂之玄。
> Cǐ liǎng zhě tóng chū ér yì míng tóng, wèi zhī xuán.

These | two | ones | same | out | yet | different | names | same, | Called | of⇆ | mystery.

▶ The two words for mystery here have different meanings. 玄 (xuán) is *dark, mysterious, unseen, withdrawn, deep.* 妙 (miào) is lighter, a *wonderful mystery.*

▶ The deep mystery of things, and their superficial appearance; the mystery and the manifested; the path and the source of the path. These are all the same but differ in name.

Mystery upon mystery,
The doorway to wonder.

> 玄之又玄，众妙之门。
> Xuán zhī yòu xuán, zhòng miào zhī mén.

Mystery | of⇆ | again | mystery, |
Many | wonderful mystery | of⇆ | door.

2

In this world, beauty is called beauty because there is ugliness.
Good is called good because there is evil.

Thus, emptiness and existence transform into each other,
Difficult and easy come from each other,
Long and short compare to each other,
High and low flow from each other,
Sounds and voices blend together in harmony,
Before and after follow each other.

Knowing this, the sage acts by doing nothing,
And teaches without saying a word.
The ten thousand things arise but he is silent.
Things grow but he takes nothing for himself.

He acts but doesn't compel.
He creates but seeks no recognition.
By not seeking recognition, he has nothing to lose.

In this world, beauty is called beauty because there is ugliness.

> 天下，皆知美之为美斯恶已。
> Tiānxià, jiē zhī měi zhī wèi měi sī è yǐ.

Under heaven, | all | know | beauty | of⇆ | as | beauty | this | hate/evil | already.

▶ As a noun, 恶 (è) means *evil*. As a verb, it means *to hate*. This verse is ambiguous, it could mean either one. We use *ugliness* because it's a better fit in English, the opposite of 美 (měi), *beauty, goodness*.

Good is called good because there is evil.

> 皆知善之为善斯不善已。
> Jiē zhī shàn zhī wéi shàn sī búshàn yǐ.

All | know | good | of⇆ | as | good | this | not good | already.

Thus, emptiness and existence transform into each other,
Difficult and easy come from each other,

> 故，有无相生，难易相成，
> Gù, yǒu wú xiāng shēng, nán yì xiāng chéng,

Therefore, | have | not have | each other | born, |
Hard | easy | each other | become,

▶ In Chinese, two opposites together can mean "this type of measurement"; for example, 难易 (nán yì), *hard easy*, can mean *difficulty*, and 长短 (cháng duǎn) *long short* can mean *length*.

Long and short compare to each other,
High and low flow from each other,

> 长短相较，高下相倾，
> Cháng duǎn xiāng jiào, gāo xià xiāng qīng,

Long | short | each other | compare, | high | low | each other | pour,

Sounds and voices blend together in harmony,
Before and after follow each other.

> 音声相和，前后相随。
> Yīn shēng xiāng hé; qiánhòu xiāng suí.

Sounds | voices | each other | harmony, |
Before | after | each other | follow.

Knowing this, the sage acts by doing nothing,
And teaches without saying a word.

> 是以圣人处无为之事，行不言之教。
> Shìyǐ | shèngrén | chǔ | wúwéi | zhī | shì, xíng bù yán zhī jiào.

Therefore | sage | implement | empty action | of⇆ | duty, |
Do | not | say | of⇆ | teach.

▸ Two important words appear here for the first time. 圣人 (shèngrén), *saintly one*, is someone who understands the way of the Dao and lives by its wisdom. And 无为 (wúwéi), *empty action*, is the way of life for the wise: doing without striving, leading without pushing, acting without an end in mind.

The ten thousand things arise but he is silent.
Things grow but he takes nothing for himself.

> 万物作焉而不辞。生而不有。
> Wànwù zuò yān ér bù cí. Shēng ér bù yǒu.

Ten thousand things/creatures | do | <!> | but | not | speech. |
Grow | yet | not | have.

He acts but doesn't compel.
He creates but seeks no recognition.

> 为而不恃。功成而弗居。
> Wéi ér bú shì. Gong chéng ér fú jū.

Make | yet | not | compel. |
Achieve | finish | yet | not | take honor.

▶ 居 (jū): typically *to live*, but here, *to accept honors given by others*

By not seeking recognition, he has nothing to lose.

> 夫唯弗居是，以不去。
> Fū wéi fú jū, shìyǐ bú qù.

So | only | not | take honor, | therefore | not | leave.

3

Don't honor good men, and the people will not strive.
Don't value rare goods, and the people will not steal.
Don't show off valuables, and the peoples' hearts will not be confused.

Thus, the wise ruler empties minds and fills stomachs,
Weakens ambitions and strengthens bones.

Make sure the people have no knowledge and no desire.
Those who have knowledge will not dare to act!

Do without doing, and all will be peaceful.

Don't honor good men, and the people will not strive.

> 不尚贤，使民不争。
> Bú shàng xián, shǐ mín bù zhēng.

Not | value | virtuous, | let | citizens | no | fight.

▸ This chapter offers advice to leaders, but the advice applies just as well to the individual life.

▸ 民 (mín): *subjects* or *citizens,* depending on the form of government

▸ 贤 (xián): *good*, but also *virtuous, worthy, having superior ability*

▸ 争 (zhēng): *strive* but has a negative feeling, such as *dispute, contend, fight*

Don't value rare goods, and the people will not steal.

> 不贵难得之货，使民不为盗。
> Bú guì nán dé zhī huò, shǐ mín bù wéi dào.

Not | expensive | difficult | get | of⇋ | goods, | cause | people | not | make | steal.

Don't show off valuables, and the peoples' hearts will not be confused.

> 不见可欲，使心不乱。
> Bú jiàn kě yù, shǐ xīn bú luàn.

Not | perceive | can | desire, | let | heart | no | confusion.

▸ In Chinese, 心 (xīn) is both *heart* and *mind,* the seat of feeling.

Thus, the wise ruler empties minds and fills stomachs,

> 是以圣人之治虚其心实其腹，
> Shìyǐ shèngrén zhī zhì xū qí xīn, shí qí fù,

Therefore | sage | of 与 | rule | weaken | their | hearts | fill | their | stomachs,

▸ In describing the actions of the sage in these two lines, 其 (qí) appears four times between verb and noun. It's a general pronoun and can mean *his, her, its, their* depending on context.

Weakens ambitions and strengthens bones.

> 弱其志强其骨。
> Ruò qí zhì qiáng qí gǔ.

Weak | their | purpose | strong | their | bones.

▸ 志 (zhì): *purpose, will, determination, ambition*

Make sure the people have no knowledge and no desire.

> 常使民无知无欲。
> Cháng shǐ mín wú zhī wú yù.

Often | let | people | emptiness | knowledge | emptiness | desire.

Those who have knowledge will not dare to act!

> 使夫知者不敢为也。
> Shǐ fū zhīzhě bù gǎn wéi yě.

Let | <preposition> | knowledgeable person | not | dare | do | <!>.

▸ In the kingdom, the intellectuals ("men who know") will be powerless to interfere. Within yourself, the intellect will be quieted.

Do without doing, and all will be peaceful.

> 为无为，则无不治。
> Wéiwúwéi, zé wú bú zhì.

Do without doing, | then | nothing | no/cannot | rule.

▶ 为无为 (wéi wú wéi): *do without doing*

▶ 无不治 (wú bú zhì): *nothing cannot be ruled*, a double negative, so it means "everything's under control" or "to rule peacefully."

4

Dao is a bottomless cup that need not be filled.
Profound and deep, it is the root of ten thousand things.

It blunts sharpness, loosens tangles,
Softens brightness, makes us as dust.

Deep and profound! It barely exists.

I don't know whose child it is.
It appeared before the great kings.

Dao is a bottomless cup that need not be filled.

> 道冲而用之或不盈。
> Dào chōng ér yòng zhī huò bù yíng.

Dao | bottomless cup | so | use | of⇆ | maybe | not | full.

▸ 冲 (chōng) in ancient Chinese is *a wine cup with no bottom*, resembling an endlessly flowing pipe or tube.

▸ Another possible translation: "Dao: use it like a cup that cannot be emptied." Chapter 9 says more about the virtues of not being full.

Profound and deep, it is the root of ten thousand things.

> 渊兮，似万物之宗。
> Yuān xī, shì wànwù zhī zōng.

Deep | <!> | as if | ten thousand things/creatures | of⇆ | origin/ancestor.

▸ 渊 (yuān): *deep, profound, an abyss*

It blunts sharpness, loosens tangles,

> 挫其锐，解其纷，
> Cuò qí ruì, jiě qí fēn,

Grind | his/her | sharp, | loosen | his/her | tangles,

Softens brightness, makes us as dust.

> 和其光，同其尘。
> Hé qí guāng, tóng qí chén.

Calm | his/her | brightness, | same | his/her | dust/dirt.

Deep and profound! It barely exists.

> 湛兮，似或存。
> Zhàn xī, shì huò cún.

Deep | <!>, | as if | maybe | exist.

I don't know whose child it is.

> 吾不知谁之子。
> Wú bùzhī shuí zhī zǐ.

I | don't know | who | of⇆ | child.

It appeared before the great kings.

> 象帝之先。
> Xiàng dì zhī xiān.

Image | emperor | of⇆ | before.

▶ 帝 (dì): *supreme ruler, emperor, God.* Here it refers to god-kings of heaven instead of a human ruler. The line literally reads, "before the image of the Supreme One."

5

Heaven and earth aren't kind;
To them, the ten thousand things are as straw dogs.

The sage isn't kind;
To him, the common people are as straw dogs.

Isn't the space between heaven and earth like a bellows?
It is empty but cannot be exhausted.
The more it moves, the more comes out.
The more you talk, the weaker you become.

Better to remain centered.

Heaven and earth aren't kind;

> 天地不仁;
> Tiāndì | bù | rén;

Heaven and earth | not | benevolent;

To them, the ten thousand things are as straw dogs.

> 以，万物为刍狗。
> Yǐ, | wànwù | wéi | chú | gǒu.

Thus, | ten thousand things/creatures | as if | grass | dog.

▶ In Chinese tradition, 刍狗 (chú gǒu), *grass dog*, is something that is worthless of itself, but is burned as a representation of valuable goods in honor of the dead. Traditionally, these were grass or straw fashioned into the shape of a dog and used in a ritual where they were burned to remove evil energy. A variation on this tradition still exists in China today.

The sage isn't kind;

> 圣人不仁;
> Shèngrén | bù | rén;

Sage | not | benevolent;

To him, the common people are as straw dogs.

> 以，百姓为刍狗。
> Yǐ, | bǎixìng | wéi | chú | gǒu.

Thus, | ordinary people | as if | grass | dog.

Isn't the space between heaven and earth like a bellows?

> 天地之间其犹橐籥乎。
> Tiāndì zhī jiān qí yóu tuó yuè hū.

Heaven and earth | of⇆ | interval | it | resemble | tube | bag | <!>.

▸ 橐籥 (tuó yuè): *bellows*, literally, a "tube bag"

It is empty but cannot be exhausted.

> 虚而不屈。
> Xū ér bù qū.

Empty | but | not | exhausted.

▸ 屈 (qū): in modern usage *bent*, but in Classical Chinese *emptied, exhausted*

The more it moves, the more comes out.

> 动，而愈出。
> Dòng, ér yù chū.

Move, | so | more | go out.

The more you talk, the weaker you become.

> 多言，数穷。
> Duō yán, shù qióng.

Much | speak, | speed up | impoverished.

▸ Literally, "speak a lot, quickly become exhausted."

Better to remain centered.

> 不如守中。
> Bùrú shǒu zhōng.

It would be better | guard | center.

6

The spirit of the center is called the mysterious feminine.
Its doorway is called the source of heaven and earth.

It seems to be unbroken.
Use it; it never ends.

The spirit of the center is called the mysterious feminine.

> 谷神不死是谓玄牝。
> Gǔ shén bù sǐ shì wèi xuán pìn.

Center/grain/valley | spirit | not | die | is | said | deep | female.

▶ 谷 (gǔ) has many meanings including grain, valley, and paddy, but the meaning here is *the still center, a navel, the hub of a wheel*.

▶ 神 (shén): *spirit, god*.

▶ 牝 (pìn): *a female animal*, but more broadly, *motherhood*

Its doorway is called the source of heaven and earth.

> 玄牝之门是谓天地根。
> Xuán pìn zhī mén shì wèi tiāndì gēn.

Deep | female | of⇆ | door | is | said | heaven and earth | foundation/root.

▶ What is the doorway to the center? Remember the 橐籥 (tuó yuè) from the previous chapter: a bellows open at both ends.

It seems to be unbroken.

> 绵绵若存。
> Miánmián ruò cún.

Unbroken | like this | exist.

▶ By itself 绵 (mián) means *soft*, like cotton, but 绵绵 (miánmián) means *unbroken, continuous*. Imagine an unbroken sea of clouds.

Use it; it never ends.

> 用之不勤。
> Yòng zhī bù qín.

Use | of⇆ | not | constant.

7

Heaven is eternal, earth lasts a long time,
So heaven and earth can last forever.
They don't live for themselves,
So they can live a long time.

Thus, the sage puts himself behind,
Yet finds himself in front.
Giving no thought for himself,
He survives.

Is it because he is selfless
That he can achieve selfish goals?

Heaven is eternal, earth lasts a long time,

> 天长，地久，
> Tiān cháng, dì jiǔ,

> Heaven | forever, | earth | long time,

So heaven and earth can last forever.

> 天地所以能长且久者。
> Tiāndì suǒyǐ néng cháng qiě jiǔ zhě.

> Heaven and earth | so | can | long | and | long time | such.

They don't live for themselves,
So they can live a long time.

> 以其不自生，故能长生。
> Yǐ qí bú zì shēng, gù néng cháng shēng.

> Because | him/her | no | oneself | life |
> Therefore | can | long | life.

Thus, the sage puts himself behind,
Yet finds himself in front.

> 是以圣人后其身，而身先。
> Shìyǐ shèngrén hòu qí shēn, ér shēn xiān.

> Therefore | sage | behind | his/her | self, |
> But | self | first.

Giving no thought for himself,
He survives.

> 外其身，而身存。
> Wài qí shēn, ér shēn cún.

Outside | him/her | self |
But | self | exist.

- 外其身 (wài qí shēn): *giving no thought for the self*

- 存 (cún): *exist, live, be survive, remain*

Is it because he is selfless
That he can achieve selfish goals?

> 非以其无私耶故能成其私?
> Fēi yǐ qí wúsī yé gù néng chéng qí sī?

Not true | because | him/her | selfless | <!> |
Thus | can | achieve | his/her | selfish?

- 无 (wú) here means *not*, and not the deeper *emptiness*.

- 私 (sī) is used in these two lines, it is an somewhat negative adjective meaning *private, personal, selfish*. But used here as a noun, it can mean *one's own private goals*.

8

The highest kindness is like water.
Water's kindness benefits everything, yet it doesn't strive.
It even lives in places that everyone dislikes, like the Dao.

The virtue of a home is its land,
The virtue of the heart is its depth,
The virtue of a friendship is its kindness,
The virtue of speech is its honesty,
The virtue of governing is establishing peaceful order,
The virtue of doing your duty is being competent,
The virtue of action is its timing.

When there is no striving, there is no blame.

The highest kindness is like water.

> 上善若水。
> Shàng shàn ruò shuǐ.

Top | good | like | water.

▶ 善 (shàn): *kindness, virtue, goodness*

Water's kindness benefits everything, yet it doesn't strive.

> 水善利万物，而不争。
> Shuǐ shàn lì wànwù, ér bù zhēng.

Water | good | benefit | ten thousand things/creatures, | but | not | dispute.

It even lives in places that everyone dislikes, like the Dao.

> 处众人之所恶，故几于道。
> Chù zhòngrén zhī suǒ è, gù jī yú dào.

Stay | crowd | of⇆ | that | evil, | therefore | almost | close | Dao.

The virtue of a home is its land,

> 居善地，
> Jū shàn dì,

Dwell | good | earth,

▶ These seven lines tell us about water and the Dao, and all follow the same pattern: noun + 善 (shàn) meaning *virtue* or *goodness* + adjective.

The virtue of the heart is its depth,

> 心善渊，
> Xīn shàn yuān,

Heart | good | deep,

▸ 渊 (yuān): *deep, profound, still*

The virtue of a friendship is its kindness,

> 与善仁，
> Yǔ shàn rén,

Comrade | good | kindness,

The virtue of speech is its honesty,

> 言善信，
> Yán shàn xìn,

Speak | good | truth,

The virtue of governing is establishing peaceful order,

> 政善治，
> Zhèng shàn zhì,

Politics | good | management/rule,

The virtue of doing your duty is being competent,

> 事善能，
> Shì shàn néng,

Duty | good | ability,

The virtue of action is its timing.

> 动善时。
> Dòng shàn shí.

Action | good | timing.

When there is no striving, there is no blame.

> 夫唯不争，故无尤。
> Fū wéi bù zhēng, gù wú yóu.

So | only | not | strive | then | no | blame.

9

Filling up isn't as good as knowing when to stop.
A sharp point can't be maintained for long.

When gold and jade fill a room, no one can protect it.
When wealth leads to arrogance, it invites mistakes.

Achieve success, then let it go.
This is the Dao of heaven.

Filling up isn't as good as knowing when to stop.

> 持而盈之不如其已。
> Chí ér yíng zhī bùrú qí yǐ.

Support/hold | cause | full | this | | not as good as | its | stop.

A sharp point can't be maintained for long.

> 揣而锐之不可长保。
> Chuāi ér ruì zhī bù kě cháng bǎo.

To hammer | cause | sharp | this | not | can | long | protect.

▶ 揣 (chuāi): *hammer a piece of metal to make it sharp*. In this line, it's the sharpness itself that can't be maintained, not the sharpening process.

When gold and jade fill a room, no one can protect it.

> 金玉满堂，莫之能守。
> Jīn yù mǎn táng, mò zhī néng shǒu.

Gold | jade/jewels | fill | room, | not | this | can | defend.

When wealth leads to arrogance, it invites mistakes.

> 富贵而骄，自遗其咎。
> Fùguì ér jiāo, zì yí qí jiù.

Rich | cause | arrogant, | oneself | remain | his/her | mistake.

Achieve success, then let it go.

> 功遂，身退。
> Gōng suì, shēn tuì.

Achievement | fulfill, | self | retreat.

This is the Dao of heaven.

> 天之道。
> Tiān zhī dào.

Heaven | of⇆ | Dao.

10

The body embraces the soul,
Can you not split them apart?

Concentrate the breath to become soft,
Can you be like a newborn infant?

Purify and examine your deepest thoughts,
Can you be without blemish?

Love the citizens and govern the nation,
Can you do nothing?

Open your senses to meet the world,
Can you remain calm?

See clearly in all four directions,
Can you not interfere?

Create and nurture,
Create but don't possess,
Act but don't compel,
Lead but don't dominate.

This is called the Primal De.

The body embraces the soul,
Can you not split them apart?

> 载营魄抱一，能无离乎？
> Zài yíngpò bào yī, néng wú lí hū?

Carry | soul | surround/hold | one, | can | not | separate | <!>?

▶ 抱一 (bào yī), *surround one*. When the body embraces the soul, the two become one.

Concentrate the breath to become soft,
Can you be like a newborn infant?

> 专气致柔，能婴儿乎？
> Zhuān qì zhì róu, néng yīng'ér hū?

Gather | *qi* | to | soft, | can | infant | <!>?

▶ 气 (qì), *breath*, but also *life force*. Commonly called "chi" in English.

Purify and examine your deepest thoughts,
Can you be without blemish?

> 涤除玄览，能无疵乎？
> Dí chú xuán lǎn, néng wú cī hū?

Cleanse | eliminate | mystery/deep | introspection, | can | not | flaw | <!>?

Love the citizens and govern the nation,
Can you do nothing?

> 爱民治国，能无为乎？
> Ài mín zhì guó, néng wúwéi hū?

Love | citizens | rule | nations, | can | empty action | <!>?

Open your senses to meet the world,
Can you remain calm?

> 天门开阖，能为雌乎？
> Tiānmén kāi hé, néng wéi cí hū?

The five senses | open | world, | can | be | motherly calm | <!>?

▶ 天门 (tiānmén): *heaven's door(s),* the five senses

▶ 阖 (hé): *everything, the entire family, the whole wide world*

See clearly in all four directions,
Can you not interfere?

> 明白四达，能无知乎？
> Míngbái sì dá, néng wú zhī hū?

Understand | four | reach, |
Can | not | calculating person | <!>?

▶ Literally, "... can you not be a manipulating person?"

Create and nurture,
Create but don't possess,

> 生之畜之，生而不有，
> Shēng zhī xù zhī, shēng ér bù yǒu,

Birth | it | raise | it, |
Birth | but | not | have,

Act but don't compel,
Lead but don't dominate,
This is called the Primal De.

> 为而不恃，长而不宰，是谓玄德。
> Wéi ér bú shì, zhǎng ér bù zǎi, shì wèi xuándé.

Act | but | not | compel, |
Rule/lead | but | not | dominate, |
Is | said | Primal De.

▶ In the chapter we learn about De, which might be translated as "the power of Dao in the world." It is a way of living and acting that is guided by Dao.

11

Thirty spokes share a single hub,
Its emptiness makes the cart useful.

Form clay to make a container,
Its emptiness makes the container useful.

Cut doors and windows to make a room,
Its emptiness makes the room useful.

So, a thing's existence makes it beneficial,
But emptiness makes it useful.

Thirty spokes share a single hub,
Its emptiness makes the cart useful.

> 三十辐共一毂，当其无有车之用。
> Sānshí fú gòng yī gǔ, dāng qí wú yǒu chē zhī yòng.

Thirty | spokes | together | one | hub, |
When | it's | empty | have | cart | of⇆ | use.

Form clay to make a container,
Its emptiness makes the container useful.

> 埏埴以为器，当其无有器之用。
> Shān zhí yǐwéi qì, dāng qí wú yǒu qì zhī yòng.

Mix | clay | so as | receptacle, |
When | it | empty | have | receptacle | of⇆ | use.

Cut doors and windows to make a room,
Its emptiness makes the room useful.

> 凿户牖以为室，当其无有室之用。
> Záo hù yǒu yǐwéi shì, dāng qí wú yǒu shì zhī yòng.

Chisel | door | window | so as | room, |
When | it | empty | have | room | of⇆ | use.

So, a thing's existence makes it beneficial,
But emptiness makes it useful.

> 故有之以为利，无之以为用。
> Gù yǒu zhī yǐwéi lì, wú zhī yǐwéi yòng.

Thus | exist | of⇆ | so as | beneficial, |
Empty | of⇆ | so as | use.

▸ Usually 有 (yǒu) means *to have*, but here it means *to be*.

12

The five colors can make our eyes blind.
The five tones can make our ears deaf.
The five flavors can make our mouths numb.
Horse racing and hunting can make our hearts go mad.
Rare goods can make us corrupt.

So, the sage feeds the people
And doesn't distract them.

He leaves that and chooses this.

The five colors can make our eyes blind.

> 五色令人目盲。
> Wǔ sè lìng rén mù máng.

Five | colors | cause | person | eye | blind.

▸ The five colors are green, yellow, red, white and black.

The five tones can make our ears deaf.

> 五音令人耳聋。
> Wǔ yīn lìng rén ěr lóng.

Five | tones | make | person | ear | deaf.

▸ The five tones of the pentatonic scale are C, D, E, G and A.

The five flavors can make our mouths numb.

> 五味令人口爽。
> Wǔ wèi lìng rén kǒu shuǎng.

Five | tastes | make | person | mouth | numb/cold.

▸ The five flavors are salty, bitter, sour, pungent and sweet.

▸ The last word, 爽 (shuǎng) in ancient times referred to oral disease where one loses their sense of taste; later it came to mean *the coldness of death*.

Horse racing and hunting can make our hearts go mad.

> 驰骋田猎令人心发狂。
> Chíchěng tián liè lìng rén xīn fākuáng.

Gallop | field | hunt | make | person | heart | go crazy.

Rare goods can make us corrupt.

> 难得之货令人行妨。
> Nán dé zhī huò lìng rén xíng fáng.

Difficult | get | of ⇆ | goods | make | person | go | hinder/obstruct.

So, the sage feeds the people
And doesn't distract them.

> 是以圣人为腹不为目。
> Shìyǐ shèngrén wèi fù bú wèi mù.

Therefore | sage | for | abdomen/belly | Not | for | see.

▶ Literally, this line is "therefore, the sage is for belly, not for sight." In Chinese culture, being fed is critically important, so the sage feeds the people while not allowing them to see the distractions of the world. Similar to Chapter 3: "the wise ruler empties minds and fills stomachs."

He leaves that and chooses this.

> 故去彼取此。
> Gù qù bǐ qǔ cǐ.

Thus, | give up | that | choose | this.

▶ The sage ignores external distractions (that) and chooses to feed the people (this).

13

Favor and humiliation are both frightening.
Pay attention to risk as you would to your own body.

Why do we say "favor and humiliation are both frightening"?
Favor makes you inferior.
You fear getting it and fear losing it.
This is the meaning of "favor and humiliation are both frightening."

Why do we say "pay attention to risk as you would to your own body"?
I suffer because I have a body.
If I have no body, how can I suffer?

If you can treat the world like your own body, take it.
If you can love the world like your own body, rule it.

Favor and humiliation are both frightening.

> 宠辱若惊。
> Chǒng rǔ ruò jīng.

Favor/pamper | humiliation | same as | alarm/frighten.

▶ 宠 (chǒng): *favor*, something given to you and possibly taken away later by a superior, thus emphasizing your inferiority. Like pampering a pet.

▶ 惊 (jīng): *shock, fright, surprise,* or *startle*. An alternate translation of this line might be "beware of both pampering and humiliation."

Pay attention to risk as you would to your own body.

> 贵大患若身。
> Guì dà huàn ruò shēn.

Pay attention to | big | suffering/risk | same as | body.

▶ 贵 (guì): usually *valuable, rich*, but in this context, *important*, something you must pay close attention to

▶ 患 (huàn): *trouble, danger, misfortune, risk*

▶ 身 (shēn): *body of a person or animal*. Not just a body, but a sense of self, something that must be defended. You could substitute *ego* for *self* throughout this chapter.

Why do we say "favor and humiliation are both frightening"?

> 何谓宠辱若惊?
> Héwèi chǒng rǔ ruò jīng?

What meaning | favor/pamper | humiliation | same as | alarm/frighten?

Favor makes you inferior.
You fear getting it and fear losing it.

> 宠为下。得之若惊失之若惊。
> Chǒng wéi xià. Dé zhī ruò jīng shī zhī ruò jīng.

Favor/pamper | as | low. |
Get | of⇆ | seem | frighten | lose | of⇆ | seem | frighten.

This is the meaning of "favor and humiliation are both frightening."

> 是谓宠辱若惊。
> Shì wèi chǒng rǔ ruò jīng.

Is | speak | favor/pamper | humiliation | same as | alarm/frighten.

Why do we say "pay attention to risk as you would to your own body"?

> 何谓贵大患若身？
> Héwèi guì dà huàn ruò shēn?

What mean | valuable | big | suffering | same as | body?

I suffer because I have a body.
If I have no body, how can I suffer?

> 吾所以有大患者为吾有身。及吾无身，吾有何患？
> Wú suǒyǐ yǒu dà huàn zhě wèi wú yǒu shēn.
> Jí wú wú shēn, wú yǒu hé huàn?

I | so | have | big | worries | which that is | because | I | have | body. |
If | I | no | body, | I | have | what | suffering?

If you can treat the world like your own body, take it.

> 故贵以身为天下，若可寄天下。
> Gù guì yǐ shēn wéi tiānxià, ruò kě jì tiānxià.

Therefore | valuable | as | body | act | under heaven, | so | can | rely on | under heaven.

If you can love the world like your own body, rule it.

> 爱以身为天下，若可托天下。
> Ài yǐ shēn wéi tiānxià, ruò kě tuō tiānxià.

Love | as | body | act | under heaven, | so | can | trust | under heaven.

▶ 托 (tuō): *trust*. So here, "rule it" is literally "I trust you to take care of it" and these final two lines can be summarized as "such a person can be trusted to act as a trustee of everything under heaven."

14

Look but not see, call it dim.
Listen but not hear, call it faint.
Reach but not grasp, call it slight.
These three things can't be investigated, they blend and become one.

Its top is not bright, its bottom is not dark.
Unceasing, nameless, it returns to the void.
It is the form of the formless, the image of the void.
Confusing and indistinct.

Meet it, you can't see its beginning.
Follow it, you can't see its end.

Hold fast to the ancient Dao,
Master the present moment.

Know the ancient beginning,
Remain grounded in the Dao.

Look but not see, call it dim.

> 视之不见，名曰夷。
> Shì zhī bú jiàn, míng yuē yí.

Look | of⇋ | not | see, | name | say | elusive/colorless.

Listen but not hear, call it faint.

> 听之不闻，名曰希。
> Tīng zhī bù wén, míng yuē xī.

Listen | of⇋ | not | hear, | name | say | rare/soundless.

Reach but not grasp, call it slight.

> 搏之不得，名曰微。
> Bó zhī bùdé, míng yuē wēi.

Seize | of⇋ | not | get, | name | say | tiny/shapeless.

These three things can't be investigated, they blend and become one.

> 此三者不可致诘，故混而为一。
> Cǐ sān zhě bùkě zhì jié, gù hùn ér wéi yī.

These | three | things | cannot | cause | question/interrogate, | so | blend | then | make | one.

Its top is not bright, its bottom is not dark.

> 其上不皦，其下不昧。
> Qí shàng bù jiǎo, qí xià bú mèi.

Its | up/top | not | bright, | its | down/below | not | dark.

Unceasing, nameless, it returns to the void.

> 绳绳不可名，复归于无物。
> Shéngshéng bùkě míng, fùguī yú wúwù.

Endless | cannot | name, | return | to | void.

It is the form of the formless, the image of the void,

> 是谓无状之状，无物之象，
> Shì wèi wú zhuàng zhī zhuàng, wúwù zhī xiàng,

This | say | no | appearance | of⇆ | appearance, | nothing | of⇆ | image,

Confusing and indistinct.

> 是谓惚恍。
> Shì wèi hū huǎng.

This | say | confused | absentminded/muddled.

Meet it, you can't see its beginning.
Follow it, you can't see its end.

> 迎之，不见其首。随之，不见其后。
> Yíng zhī, bú jiàn qí shǒu.
> Suí zhī, bú jiàn qí hòu.

Greet | it, | not | see | its | head. |
Follow | it, | not | see | its | end.

Hold fast to the ancient Dao,
Master the present moment.

> 执古之道，以御今之有。
> Zhí gǔ zhī dào, yǐ yù jīn zhī yǒu.

Hold | ancient | of⇆ | Dao, |
Then | master | now | of⇆ | have.

Know the ancient beginning,
Remain grounded in the Dao.

> 能知古始，是谓道纪。
> **Néng zhī gǔ shǐ, shì wèi dào jì.**

Can | know | ancient | beginning, |
Is | say | Dao | principle.

15

The ancient masters were subtle, deep, mysterious.
We can't understand their mysterious depths.

We can't understand them,
But we must try to describe them.

Cautious, as if crossing a winter stream.
Watchful, as if afraid of threats from all sides.
Respectful, like a visiting guest.
Yielding, like the breakup of winter ice.
Simple and honest, like an uncarved block.
Wide and open, like a valley.
Murky, like muddy water.

Who can take muddy water, and through stillness make it clear?
Who can take what is tranquil, and through movement bring it to life?

Maintain the Dao, you won't want to be full.
If you're not full, there is no need to be renewed.

The ancient masters were subtle, deep, mysterious.
We can't understand their mysterious depths.

> 古之善为士者，微妙玄通。深不可识。
> Gǔ zhī shàn wéi shì zhě, wéimiào xuán tōng. Shēn bùkě shí.

Ancient | of⇆ | good at | as | scholar | he/she who is, | subtle | deep | pass through. |
Deep | cannot | understand.

We can't understand them,
But we must try to describe them.

> 夫唯不可识，故强为之容。
> Fū wéi bùkě shí, gù qiáng wéi zhī róng.

So | only | cannot | understand, |
So | reluctant | as | of⇆ | describe.

▸ Many lines in DDJ begin with 夫 (fū), which can either mean *man* (that is, an ordinary working man) or *so/therefore*. These two meanings may seem completely different, but in informal English we do something similar when we say "Man, it's hot today!"

Cautious, as if crossing a winter stream.
Watchful, as if afraid of threats from all sides.

> 豫兮若冬涉川。犹兮若畏四邻。
> Yù xī ruò dōng shè chuān. Yóu xī ruò wèi sì lín.

Hesitant/cautious | <!> | like | winter | cross | stream. |
Wary | <!> | like | fear | four | neighbors.

▸ that is, neighbors attacking from the north, south, east and west.

Respectful, like a visiting guest.
Yielding, like the breakup of winter ice.

> 俨兮，其若容。 涣兮，若冰之将释。
> Yǎn xī, qí ruò róng. Huàn xī, ruò bīng zhī jiāng shì.

Respectful | <!>, | him/her | same | looks. |
Scattered | <!>, | like | ice | of⇆ | about to | release.

Simple and honest, like an uncarved block.
Wide and open, like a valley.
Murky, like muddy water.

> 敦兮，其若朴。旷兮，其若谷。混兮，其若浊。
> Dūn xī, qí ruò pǔ. Kuàng xī, qí ruò gǔ. Hún xī, qí ruò zhuó.

Honest | <!>, | him/her | like | rough/simple. |
Broad | <!>, | him/her | like | valley. |
Turbid | <!>, | him/her | like | muddy.

Who can take muddy water, and through stillness make it clear?

> 孰能浊，以静之徐清？
> Shú néng zhuó, yǐ jìng zhī xú qīng?

Who/what | can | muddy, | with | quiet | of⇆ | calm | clear?

Who can take what is tranquil, and through movement bring it to life?

> 孰能安，以久动之徐生？
> Shú néng ān, yǐ jiǔ dòng zhī xú shēng?

Who/what | can | peaceful, | with | time passage | move/bring | of⇆ | calm | birth?

Maintain the Dao, you won't want to be full.

> 保此道者，不欲盈。
> Bǎo cǐ dào zhě, bú yù yíng.

Protect/keep up | this | Dao | person, | not | desire | full.

If you're not full, there is no need to be renewed.

> 夫唯不盈，故能蔽不新成。
> Fū wéi bù yíng, gù néng bì bù xīn chéng.

So | for | not | full, | therefore | can | cover/shield | not | new | become.

16

Become completely empty,
Maintain true stillness.

The ten thousand creatures all arise, and I watch them return,
Swarming, they return to their source.

Returning to the source is called stillness,
It's called returning to nature,

Returning to nature is called unchanging,
Knowing the unchanging is called insight.

Not knowing the unchanging is reckless and leads to misfortune.
Knowing the unchanging leads to tolerance.

Tolerance leads to justice,
Justice leads to royalty,
Royalty leads to Heaven,
Heaven leads to Dao,
Dao leads to eternity.

All your life, you're in no danger.

Become completely empty,
Maintain true stillness.

> 致虚极，守静笃。
> Zhì xū jí, shǒu jìng dǔ.

Towards | empty | extreme, | abide | quiet | deep.

The ten thousand creatures all arise, and I watch them return,

> 万物并作，吾以观复，
> Wànwù bìng zuò, wú yǐ guān fù,

Ten thousand things/creatures | all | arise, | I | thus | observe | return,

Swarming, they return to their source.

> 夫物芸芸，各复归其根。
> Fū wù yúnyún, gè fù guī qí gēn.

So | creature | numerous/varied, | each | repeatedly | return | its | root.

Returning to the source is called stillness,
It's called returning to nature,

> 归根曰静，是谓复命，
> Guīgēn yuē jìng, shì wèi fù mìng,

Return root | called | quiet, |
Is | speak | return | nature,

▶ 命 (mìng): *life, destiny, fate, mandate.* Nature is life in harmony.

Returning to nature is called unchanging,
Knowing the unchanging is called insight.

> 复命曰常，知常曰明。
> Fù mìng yuē cháng, zhī cháng yuē míng.

Return | nature | speak | unchanging, |
Know | unchanging | speak | understand.

▶ The key word here is 常 (cháng). Originally it was a measurement of clothing. Later it came to mean *unchanging*, but also *common* or *frequent*, so it has the sense of something which is everlasting and eternally unchanging.

Not knowing the unchanging is reckless and leads to misfortune,
Knowing the unchanging leads to tolerance.

> 不知常妄作凶，知常容。
> Bù zhī cháng wàng zuò xiōng, zhī cháng róng.

Not | knowing | unchanging | foolish | bring | terrible, |
Know | unchanging | allow/tolerate.

Tolerance leads to justice,
Justice leads to royalty,
Royalty leads to Heaven,
Heaven leads to Dao,
Dao leads to eternity.

> 容乃公，公乃王，王乃天，天乃道，道乃久。
> Róng nǎi gōng, gōng nǎi wáng, wáng nǎi tiān, tiān nǎi dào, dào nǎi jiǔ.

Tolerance | thus | fair, |
Fair | thus | king, |
King | thus | sky/heaven, |
Sky/heaven | thus | Dao, |
Dao | thus | long time.

▶ These five lines all have the same simple form, just two words connected with 乃 (nǎi). 乃 means *leads to, beginning, then is,* or *like this*, but also can mean *expressing two contradictory or conflicting ideas.*

▶ In the first line, 公 (gōng) means *fair, equitable* and *honorable*, but also means *public* or *state-owned*. So this could be advice to a ruler, referring to the fair administration of the state.

All your life, you're in no danger.

> 没身不殆。
> Mò shēn bú dài.

Entire/whole | body/life | no | danger.

17

The greatest ruler is barely known to the people.
Next, one who is loved.
Next, one who is feared.
Next, one who is ridiculed.

If the ruler doesn't trust, then the people will have no trust.

Relaxed, he rarely gives orders!

When tasks are completed and duties fulfilled,
The common people all say, "This is our natural way."

The greatest ruler is barely known to the people.

> 太上下知有之。
> Tàishàng xià zhī yǒu zhī.

Superior | below | know | have | it.

Next, one who is loved.
Next, one who is feared.
Next, one who is ridiculed.

> 其次，亲而誉之。其次，畏之。其次，侮之。
> Qícì, qīn ér yù zhī. Qícì, wèi zhī. Qícì, wǔ zhī.

Next, | parental love, | therefore | praise | it. |
Next, | fear | it. |
Next, | ridicule | it.

If the ruler doesn't trust, then the people will have no trust.

> 信不足焉，有不信焉。
> Xìn bùzú yān, yǒu bú xìn yān.

Trust | inadequate | <!>, | have | no | trust | <!>.

Relaxed, he rarely gives orders!

> 悠兮，其贵言。
> Yōu xī, qí guì yán.

Leisurely/laid back | <!>, | his | valuable | talk.

▸ Literally, the ruler's speech is 贵 (guì), *expensive, precious*; his words are expensive so he uses them sparingly.

When tasks are completed and duties fulfilled,
The common people all say, "This is our natural way."

> 功成事遂，百姓皆谓我自然。
> Gōng chéng shì suì, bǎixìng jiē wèi wǒ zìrán.

Achievement | completed | duty | pass, |
Hundred families | all | say, | I/we | natural.

▶ 百姓 (bǎixìng): *hundred families*. This refers to all the family names in Chinese, so, it's a way of saying *everyone*. There were actually several hundred different family names.

▶ The last part, 我自然 (wǒ zìrán) is literally "I/my natural way" meaning "I feel that this is the natural way" or "This is my natural way." An alternate translation would be "I did it."

18

When natural order is abandoned,
There is kindness and morality.

When intelligence and intellect appear,
There is great deception.

When the six kinships are not in harmony,
Children show piety to their parents.

When nations and families fall into darkness and confusion,
There are loyal ministers.

When natural order is abandoned,
There is kindness and morality.

> 大道废，有仁义。
> Dàdào fèi, yǒu rén yì.

Natural order | discard, | have | benevolent/humane | righteousness.

▶ This chapter sharply contrasts the way of Dao with the rigid set of rules offered by Confucius. Confucius held to a moral philosophy of the family structure, as compared to Daoism which is a natural philosophy of all existence.

▶ 大道 (dà dào): the meaning here is *the highest order or political system*, not "the great Dao."

▶ 仁 (rén): *humanity's social and moral sentiments*

▶ 义 (yì): *necessary moral and ethical decisions*

When intelligence and intellect appear,
There is great deception.

> 智慧出，有大伪。
> Zhì huì chū, yǒu dà wěi.

Intelligence | intellect | leave/appear, |
Have | great | fake.

▶ 智 (zhì) and 慧 (huì) both refer to an intellectual sort of intelligence.

▶ 出 (chū) has the common meaning of *to leave*, but it can also mean the opposite, *to appear* or *to take up a post*. This seems to be the way it's used here, especially because it's a better fit with the other lines in the chapter. But some scholars have taken it the other way and translated this as "when wisdom disappears there is great deception."

When the six kinships are not in harmony,
Children show piety to their parents.

> 六亲不和，有孝慈。
> Liù qīn bù hé, yǒu xiào cí.

Six | kinships | not | harmony, |
Have | filial piety | kindness.

▶ Laozi is probably referring to the relationships of father with son, older brother with younger brother, and husband with wife. However, there are many other relationships in Chinese culture, and Confucius set out detailed rules for each. As this chapter points out, such rules are only needed when the Dao is abandoned.

When nations and families fall into darkness and confusion,
There are loyal ministers.

> 国家昏乱，有忠臣。
> Guójiā hūn luàn, yǒu zhōng chén.

Nation | twilight | chaos, |
Have | loyal | minsters.

19

Renounce holiness, abandon cleverness,
And the people benefit a hundredfold.

Renounce morality, abandon ethics,
And the people return to being kind and devoted children.

Renounce cleverness, abandon profit,
And thieves won't exist.

These three make a civil society, but it isn't enough.
So let people believe in these:
Maintain simplicity, embrace plainness.
Less selfishness, fewer desires.

Renounce holiness, abandon cleverness,
And the people benefit a hundredfold.

> 绝圣，弃智，民利百倍。
> Jué shèng, qì zhì, mín lì bǎibèi.

Cut off | holy, | reject | smart/clever, |
People | favorable/lucky | hundred times.

Renounce morality, abandon ethics,
And the people return to being kind and devoted children.

> 绝仁，弃义，民复孝慈。
> Jué rén, qì yì, mín fù xiào cí.

Cut off | benevolence, | reject | righteousness, |
People | return to | filial piety | kindness.

Renounce cleverness, abandon profit,
And thieves won't exist.

> 绝巧，弃利，盗贼无有。
> Jué qiǎo, qì lì, dàozéi wú yǒu.

Cut off | cleverness, | abandon | favorable/profitable/beneficial, |
Thief | no | exist.

These three make a civil society, but it isn't enough.

> 此三者以为文，不足。
> Cǐ sān zhě yǐwéi wén, bùzú.

These | three | things | use as | provision/rule | insufficient.

So let people believe in these:

> 故令有所属。
> Gù lìng yǒu suǒshǔ.

So | command/let/ask | have/exist | attach to.

Maintain simplicity, embrace plainness.
Less selfishness, fewer desires.

> 见素，抱朴。少私，寡欲。
> Jiàn sù, bào pǔ. Shǎo sī, guǎ yù.

Keep | simple, | embrace | plain. |
Few | personal, | few | desires.

20

Renounce learning, avoid suffering.

How far apart are "yes" and "yeah"?
How similar are good and evil?

Should we fear what others fear?
It's been like this since ancient times, it never ends!

Crowds of people are excited,
As if going to the sacrifice feast,
As if climbing terraces in the spring.

I alone am still and give no sign.
Like a newborn infant not yet a child.
So tired, with nowhere to return to!

Everyone has more than they need, but I have nothing.
So confused! Ah, I have the heart of a fool.

Common people see clearly; I alone am dazed.
Common people look sharply; I alone am simple.
They are boundless like the sea, and endless like the wind.
Everyone is shrewd; I alone am clumsy.

I alone am different from the people,
Because I value the mother of all.

Renounce learning, avoid suffering.

> 绝学, 无忧。
> Jué xué, wú yōu.

Cut off | learning, | not have | sadness.

▶ This line could fit better at the end of Chapter 19. The original manuscript ran several chapters together, so it's uncertain which chapter this should be in.

How far apart are "yes" and "yeah"?

> 唯之与阿相去几何？
> Wéi zhī yǔ ā xiāngqù jǐhé?

Yes | of⇆ | versus | careless acceptance | separated by distance | how much?

▶ 唯 (wéi) is a formal and respectful "yes". 阿 (ā) is an informal "yeah" which could be interpreted as "no," making it consistent with the following line.

How similar are good and evil?

> 善之与恶相去若何？
> Shàn zhī yǔ è xiāngqù ruò hé?

Good | of⇆ | with | evil | difference | like | how?

Should we fear what others fear?

> 人之所畏不可不畏？
> Rén zhī suǒ wèi bùkěbù wèi?

People | of⇆ | about | fear | cannot not be | fear?

> This line reads best as a question, even though the Chinese reads as a statement: "What the people fear has to be feared."

It's been like this since ancient times, it never ends!

> 荒兮，其未央哉。
> Huāng xī, qí wèi yāng zāi.

Faraway/ancient | <!>, | its | not | finish | <!>.

> Starting with this line, Laozi starts to poke fun at himself, portraying himself as others might see him.

Crowds of people are excited,
As if going to the sacrifice feast,
As if climbing terraces in the spring.

> 众人熙熙，如享太牢，如春登台。
> Zhòngrén xīxī, rú xiǎng tàiláo, rú chūn dēng tái.

Crowd of people | thriving/prosperous, |
As if | enjoy | Tailao festival, |
As if | spring | climb | terrace.

> 太牢 (Tàiláo): a major feast where sheep, pigs, and ox were ritually sacrificed and eaten

> 台 (tái): a man-made hill with paths cut into in the side, leading up to a plateau at the top from which to view the surrounding landscape

I alone am still and give no sign.

> 我独泊兮其未兆。
> Wǒ dú bó xī qí wèi zhào.

I | only | calm/indifferent | <!> | it | not | omen.

Like a newborn infant not yet a child.

> 如婴儿之未孩。
> Rú yīng'ér zhī wèi hái.

Like | infant child | of⇄ | not | giggling.

So tired, with nowhere to return to!

> 儽儽兮，若无所归。
> Lěilěi xī, ruò wú suǒ guī.

Very tired | <!>, | as if | without | of | return.

Everyone has more than they need, but I have nothing.

> 众人皆有余，而我独若遗。
> Zhòngrén jiē yǒu yú, ér wǒ dú ruò yí.

Crowd of people | everybody | has | surplus, | but | I | only | like | insufficient.

So confused! Ah, I have the heart of a fool.

> 沌沌兮，我愚人之心也哉。
> Dùndùn xī, Wǒ yú rén zhī xīn yě zāi.

Confused | <!>, | I | stupid | person | of⇄ | heart | ah | <!>.

Common people see clearly; I alone am dazed.

> 俗人昭昭，我独若昏。
> Súrén zhāozhāo, wǒ dú ruò hūn.

Common people | clear/obvious, | I | only | like | dull/stupid.

Common people look sharply; I alone am simple.

> 俗人察察，我独闷闷。
> Súrén cháchá, wǒ dú mènmèn.

Common people | scrutinize/look harshly, | I | alone | generous/simple/honest.

They are boundless like the sea, and endless like the wind.

> 澹兮其若海，飂兮若无止。
> Dàn xī qí ruò hǎi, liù xī ruò wú zhǐ.

Vast/expanse | <!> | they | like | sea, | wind | <!> | like | not | stop.

Everyone is shrewd; I alone am clumsy.

> 众人皆有以，而我独顽似鄙。
> Zhòngrén jiē yǒu yǐ, ér wǒ dú wán shì bǐ.

Crowd of people | all | have | useful/capable, | but | I | alone | stubborn/foolish | appear | boorish/clumsy.

I alone am different from the people,
Because I value the mother of all.

> 我独异于人，而贵食母。
> Wǒ dú yì yú rén, ér guì shí mǔ.

I | alone | different/strange | from | people, |
Because | rich/valuable | everything on the earth | mother.

▶ 母 (mǔ): *mother*, but refers here to the Dao. The last line could be "but I am rich because of the Dao."

21

The greatest De is possible only by following the Dao.

Dao is indistinct and blurry.

Blurry and indistinct! Inside is appearance.
Indistinct and blurry! Inside are things.

Obscure and dark! Inside is essence.
Its essence is truth. Inside is trust.

Since ancient times its name is not lost,
So I see the ancestor of the many.

How do I know this is the ancestor of the many?
Through this.

The greatest De is possible only by following the Dao.

> 孔德之容唯道是从。
> Kǒng dé zhī róng wéi dào shì cóng.

Great | De | of⇆ | appearance | only | Dao | is | followed.

▶ 德 (dé): *a way of life in harmony with Dao*, see the next section for more on this. This chapter gives some insight into how Dao forms the world.

Dao is indistinct and blurry.

> 道之为物唯恍唯惚。
> Dào zhī wéi wù wéi huǎng wéi hū.

Dao | of⇆ | as | things | only | indistinct | only | confused.

▶ How does the Dao appear? 恍 (huǎng) is *indistinct, seemingly, absent minded*; 惚 (hū) is *vague, blurry, dim*.

Blurry and indistinct! Inside is appearance.

> 忽兮恍兮，其中有象。
> Hū xī huǎng xī, qízhōng yǒu xiàng.

Confused | <!> | indistinct | <!>, | among them | has | image/shape/appearance.

Indistinct and blurry! Inside are things.

> 恍兮忽兮，其中有物。
> Huǎng xī hū xī, qízhōng yǒu wù.

Indistinct | <!> | confused | <!>, | among them | have | things/creatures.

Obscure and dark! Inside is essence.

> 窈兮冥兮，其中有精。
> Yǎo xī míng xī, qízhōng yǒu jīng.

Obscure | <!> | gloomy/dark | <!>, | among them | has | refined spirit.

▶ 精 (jīng): *life force, essence, spirit, seed, semen.*

Its essence is truth. Inside is trust.

> 其精什真，其中有信。
> Qí jīng shén zhēn, qízhōng yǒu xìn.

Its | essence | greatly | real, | among them | has | trust.

Since ancient times its name is not lost.

> 自古及今，其名不去。
> Zìgǔ jí jīn, qí míng bú qù.

Since ancient times | to | now, | its | name/fame | not | gone.

So I see the ancestor of the many.

> 以阅众甫。
> Yǐ yuè zhòng fǔ.

Thus | observe | crowd/masses | father.

▶ 众 (zhòng): *crowd*, but could be a way of saying "the ten thousand things"

How do I know this is the ancestor of the many?
Through this.

> 吾何以知众甫之状哉？以此。
> Wú héyǐ zhī zhòng fǔ zhī zhuàng zāi? Yǐ cǐ.

I | how | know | crowd | father | of ⇆ | appearance | <!>? | Through | this.

▶ What's "this"— the Dao? The things of the world? The words you are reading?

22

Yielding brings wholeness,
Bending brings straightness,
Emptying brings fullness,

Decaying brings renewal,
Diminishing brings gain,
Exceeding brings confusion.

Thus the sage embraces the One
And serves as an example to the world.

He doesn't display himself, so he appears.
He doesn't promote himself, so he succeeds.
He doesn't boast, so he becomes famous.
He doesn't brag, so he remains a long time.

Because he doesn't fight,
No one under heaven can fight against him.

The ancients say: those who yield become whole.
How can these words be wrong?
True wholeness will return to you.

Yielding brings wholeness,
Bending brings straightness,
Emptying brings fullness,

> 曲则全，枉则直，洼则盈，
> Qū zé quán, wǎng zé zhí, wā zé yíng,

Yield | then | whole, |
Bend | then | straight, |
Hollow | then | full,

Decaying brings renewal,
Diminishing brings gain,
Exceeding brings confusion.

> 弊则新，少则得，多则惑。
> Bì zé xīn, shǎo zé dé, duō zé huò.

Bad/damaged | then | new, |
Few | then | gain/success, |
Much | then | confusion.

Thus the sage embraces the One
And serves as an example to the world.

> 是以圣人抱一为天下式。
> Shìyǐ shèngrén bào yī wéi tiānxià shì.

Therefore | sage | embraces | one |
Serve as | the world | pattern.

▶ 式 (shì): *type, form, pattern, style*, a *template to follow.* Originally, orienting the constellations around a fixed unmoving center.

He doesn't display himself, so he appears.
He doesn't promote himself, so he succeeds.

> 不自见，故明。不自是，故彰。
> Bú zì xiàn, gù míng. Bú zì shì, gù zhāng.

Not | oneself | see/perceive/meet, | so | wise/appear. |
Not | oneself | right/correct, | so | clear/obvious.

He doesn't boast, so he becomes famous.
He doesn't brag, so he remains a long time.

> 不自伐，故有功。不自矜，故长。
> Bú zì fá, gù yǒu gōng. Bú zì jīn, gù cháng.

Not | oneself | proud, | so | has | merit/fame. |
Not | oneself | arrogant, | so | long.

Because he doesn't fight,
No one under heaven can fight against him.

> 夫唯不争，故天下莫能与之争。
> Fū wéi bù zhēng, gù tiānxià mò néng yǔ zhī zhēng.

So | only | not | fight, |
Thus | under heaven | not | able | with | of 与 | fight.

The ancients say: those who yield become whole.

> 古之所谓曲则全者。
> Gǔ zhī suǒwèi qū zé quán zhě.

Ancient | of 与 | so-called | bent/wrong | then | whole | those who.

How can these words be wrong?

> 岂虚言哉?
> Qǐ xū yán zāi?

How | false | speak | <!>?

True wholeness will return to you.

> 诚全而归之。
> Chéng quán ér guī zhī.

Honest/true | whole/all | therefore | return to/bring back | it/them.

23

Nature's words are few.
So, strong winds don't last the entire morning,
Sudden rains don't last all day.

Who makes these things? Heaven and earth.
Even heaven and earth can't maintain them forever,
So how can people do it?

So, engage with Dao, and become one with Dao.
Engage with De, and become one with De.
Engage with loss, and become one with loss.

Become one with Dao, and Dao welcomes you.
Become one with De, and De welcomes you.
Become one with loss, and loss welcomes you.

If you aren't worthy of trust, others won't trust you.

Nature's words are few.
So, strong winds don't last the entire morning,
Sudden rains don't last all day.

> 希言自然。故飘风不终朝，骤雨不终日。
> Xī yán zìrán. Gù piāofēng bù zhōng zhāo, zhòuyǔ bù zhōng rì.

Rare | speak | natural. |
Thus | whirlwind | not | all | morning, |
Sudden rain | not | all | day.

Who makes these things? Heaven and earth.

> 孰为此者？天地。
> Shú wéi cǐ zhě? Tiāndì.

Who | makes | these | things? | Heaven and earth.

Even heaven and earth can't maintain them forever,
So how can people do it?

> 天地尚不能久，而况于人乎？
> Tiāndì shàng bù néng jiǔ, ér kuàng yú rén hū?

Heaven and earth | even | not | able | long time, |
And so | not to mention | about | people | <!>?

So, engage with Dao, and become one with Dao.

> 故从事于道者，道者同于道。
> Gù cóngshì yú dào zhě, dào zhě tóng yú dào.

Thus, | engage | to | Dao | he/she, | Dao | he/she | same | with/to | Dao.

Engage with De, and become one with De.
Engage with loss, and become one with loss.

> 德者，同于德。失者，同于失。
> Dé zhě, tóng yú dé. Shī zhě, tóng yú shī.

De | he/she, | same | with/to | De. |
Lose | he/she, | same | with/to | lose.

▶ 失 (shī) appears in this chapter as a negative counterpoint to Dao and De. We translate it as *lose/loss*, but try substituting these other meanings: *fail, mistake, mishap, error, miss*

Become one with Dao, and Dao welcomes you.

> 同于道者，道亦乐得之。
> Tóng yú dào zhě, dào yì lè dé zhī.

Same | with/to | Dao | he/she, | Dao | also | happy | get | he/she.

Become one with De, and De welcomes you.

> 同于德者，德亦乐得之。
> Tóng yú dé zhě, dé yì lè dé zhī.

Same | with | De | he/she, | De | also | happy | get | he/she.

Become one with loss, and loss welcomes you.

> 同于失者，失亦乐得之。
> Tóng yú shī zhě, shī yì lè dé zhī.

Same | with | lose/mistake | he/she, | lose/mistake | also | happy | get | he/she.

If you aren't worthy of trust, others won't trust you.

> 信不足，焉有不信焉。
> Xìn bùzú, yān yǒu bú xìn yān.

Trust | insufficient, | then | have | not | trust | <!>.

24

One who stands on tiptoe doesn't really stand.
One who strides doesn't really walk.
One who is narrowminded doesn't have a clear view.
One who is self-righteous misses the obvious.

One who boasts doesn't achieve.
One who brags doesn't endure.

One who lives in Dao calls these
Leftover food, big belly.
People don't like them.
So, one who has Dao avoids them.

One who stands on tiptoe doesn't really stand.
One who strides doesn't really walk.

> 企者不立。跨者不行。
> Qǐ zhě bú lì. Kuà zhě bù xíng.

Stand on tiptoe | he/she | not | stand. |
Stride/ride | he/she | not | walk.

One who is narrowminded doesn't have a clear view.
One who is self-righteous misses the obvious.

> 自见者不明。自是者不彰。
> Zì xiàn zhě bù míng. Zì shì zhě bù zhāng.

Oneself | opinionated | he/she | not | understand clearly. |
Oneself | correct | he/she | not | obvious/manifest.

▶ 是 (shì) means *correct*, but here, a better translation is *acting as if one is correct*; puffing yourself up, promoting your own views, being self-righteous.

One who boasts doesn't achieve.
One who brags doesn't endure.

> 自伐者无功。自矜者不长。
> zì fá zhě wú gōng. Zì jīn zhě bù cháng.

Oneself | stab/boast | him/her | no | achievement/merit. |
Oneself | conceited | he/she | not | long.

▶ The last character here, 长, can be read either as the adjective cháng meaning *long*, or as the verb zhǎng meaning *to lead*, so this could have another meaning: "One who brags cannot lead."

One who lives in Dao calls these

> 其在道也曰
> Qí zài dào yě yuē

He/she | at/with | Dao | <!> | speak

Leftover food, big belly.
People don't like them.

> 余食，赘行。物或恶之。
> Yú shí, zhuì xíng. Wù huò wù zhī.

Surplus | food | excessive | body shape. | Things/creatures | perhaps | hate/detest | it.

▶ 余食 (yú shí): *excess food, inedible scraps*

▶ 赘行 (zhuì xíng): *a flabby body shape caused by overeating*

▶ The second line is, literally, "These things are probably disliked," referring to the unpleasantness of the things in the previous line, and contrasting nicely with the next line.

So, one who has Dao avoids them.

> 故，有道者不处。
> Gù, yǒu dào zhě bù chǔ.

So, | have | Dao | he/she | not | stay/stop/live in.

25

Something formless appeared,
Before the birth of heaven and earth.

Quiet! Sparse!
It stands alone, unchanging.
It moves everywhere endlessly,
It could be the mother of the world.

I don't know its name;
Its symbol is Dao.
If I had to name it, I would call it great.

Greatness speaks of departure.
Departure speaks of distance.
Distance speaks of returning.

Dao is great, Heaven is great,
Earth is great, the king is also great.
In this land are four great ones,
And the king is one of them!

People obey earth,
Earth obeys heaven,
Heaven obeys Dao,
Dao obeys what is natural.

Something formless appeared,
Before the birth of heaven and earth.

> 有物混成，先天地生。
> Yǒu wù hǔn chéng, xiān tiān dì shēng.

Have | thing | muddled/mixed up | appears, |
Before/first | sky | earth | born.

Quiet! Sparse!
It stands alone, unchanging.

> 寂兮，寥兮，独立不改。
> Jì xī, liáo xī, dú lì bù gǎi.

Quiet | <!>, | sparse | <!>, |
Alone | stand | not | change.

▶ 寥 (liáo): *sparse; something that's few in number but spread over a large area*

It moves everywhere endlessly,
It could be the mother of the world.

> 周行而不殆，可以为天下母。
> Zhōu xíng ér bú dài, kěyǐ wéi tiānxià mǔ.

Cycle | move | but | not | idle/relax, |
Can | serve as | under heaven | mother.

▶ 周 (zhōu): *something that moves in cycles.*

I don't know its name;
Its symbol is Dao.

> 吾不知其名；字之曰道。
> Wú bùzhī qí míng; zì zhī yuē dào.

I | don't know | its | name; |
Word | of ⇆ | say | Dao.

▶ 字 (zì) means *word* but specifically, the Chinese character for that word. So, "I don't know its name, but its symbol is 道 (dào)."

If I had to name it, I would call it great.

> 强为之名，曰大。
> Qiáng wéi zhī míng, yuē dà.

Reluctant/unconvincing | for | of ⇆ | name, | speak | great/big.

Greatness speaks of departure,
Departure speaks of distance,
Distance speaks of returning.

> 大曰逝，逝曰远，远曰反。
> Dà yuē shì, shì yuē yuǎn, yuǎn yuē fǎn.

Big/great | say | die/depart, |
Die/depart | say | far off, |
Far off | say | turn around.

▶ These three lines are concise but hard to translate. They're of the form A 曰 B, where 曰 (yuē) is *say, speak, call, name*. So they might read "Greatness is called departure," etc.

Dao is great, Heaven is great,
Earth is great, the king is also great.

> 故道大，天大，地大，王亦大。
> Gù dào dà, tiān dà, dì dà, wáng yì dà.

Therefore | Dao | great, | heaven | great, |
Earth | great, | king | also | great.

▶ 王 (wáng) means *king*. Some have translated it here as *sage* or *wise man*, but that's unlikely because other words could have been used for that.

In this land are four great ones,
And the king is one of them!

> 域中有四大，而王居其一焉。
> Yù zhōng yǒu sì dà, ér wáng jū qí yī yān.

Region | among | have | four | great, |
Whereas | king | have/be | their | one | <!>.

People obey earth,

Earth obeys heaven,

Heaven obeys Dao,

Dao obeys what is natural.

> 人法地，地法天，天法道，道法自然。
> Rén fǎ dì, dì fǎ tiān, tiān fǎ dào, dào fǎ zìrán.

People | obey/law | earth, |
Earth | obey/law | heaven, |
Heaven | obey/law | Dao, |
Dao | obey/law | natural.

▶ 法 (fǎ) as a noun means *law* or *rule*, but as a verb it can mean *obey, follow, emulate, use as a model for one's behavior*.

26

Heavy is the source of light,
Stillness is the master of impatience.

So, the sage travels all day,
And never leaves his supply wagon.

Despite glorious sights, the sage lives apart.
This is how he transcends them.

How can the master of ten thousand chariots
Act lightly in public?

Act lightly, lose the source.
Act with haste, lose the throne.

Heavy is the source of light,
Stillness is the master of impatience.

> 重为轻根，静为躁君。
> Zhòng wéi qīng gēn, jìng wéi zào jūn.

Heavy | as | light | root, |
Quiet | as | impatient | ruler.

So, the sage travels all day,
And never leaves his supply wagon.

> 是以圣人终日行，不离辎重。
> Shìyǐ shèngrén zhōngrì xíng, bù lí zī zhòng.

Therefore | sage | all day | walk, |
Not | leave | supply cart | heavy.

Despite glorious sights, the sage lives apart.

> 虽有荣观，燕处超然。
> Suī yǒu róng guān, yàn chù chāorán.

Even though | has | glorious | sights, | swallow (bird)/comfort/ease | lives | to pass or cross.

▸ 燕 (yàn) is a *swallow*, in Chinese culture a bird that is a symbol of peace and safety. Here, it's another way to refer to the sage.

How can the master of ten thousand chariots
Act lightly in public?

> 奈何万乘之主而以身轻天下？
> Nàihé wàn chéng zhī zhǔ ér yǐ shēn qīng tiānxià?

Can | ten thousand | chariots | of ⇆ | master |
Yet/but | use | body | light/frivolous | under heaven?

Act lightly, lose the source.
Act with haste, lose the throne.

> 轻，则失本。躁，则失君。
> Qīng, zé shī běn. Zào, zé shī jūn.

Light/friviolous, | then | lose | root. |
Impatient, | then | lose | kingship.

27

A good traveler leaves no tracks.
A good speaker is without flaw or disgrace.
A good accountant needs no counting tokens.
A good door has no bolt, but it can't be opened.
A good binding has no rope, but it can't be loosened.

Thus the sage always rescues people, so no one is abandoned.
The sage always preserves things, so nothing is abandoned.
This is called ancient wisdom.

So, a good person is the teacher of a bad one,
And a bad person is a lesson for a good one.
If no respect for the teacher, then no care for the lesson.

Even with wisdom there is great confusion.
This is called the essence of mystery.

A good traveler leaves no tracks.
A good speaker is without flaw or disgrace.

> 善行无辙迹。善言无瑕谪。
> Shàn xíng wú zhé jī. Shàn yán wú xiá zhé.

Good | travel | not have | wagon rut | track. |
Good | speak | not have | flaw | punish/blame.

▶ This translation is concise and fits the rhythm of the lines around it. A more accurate but wordy version would be "A good speaker makes no mistakes and invites no criticism."

A good accountant needs no counting tokens.
A good door has no bolt, but it can't be opened.

> 善数不用筹策。善闭无关楗而不可开。
> Shàn shǔ bùyòng chóucè. Shàn bì wú guān jiàn ér bù kě kāi.

Good | count/math | no need for | instruments used for calculation. |
Good | shut/block | not have | close | door bolt | yet | not | can | open.

A good binding has no rope, but it can't be loosened.

> 善结无绳约，而不可解。
> Shàn jié wú shéng yuē, ér bùkě jiě.

Good | knot | not have | rope | tie, | yet | cannot | loosen.

Thus the sage always rescues people, so no one is abandoned.

> 是以圣人常善救人，故无弃人。
> Shìyǐ shèngrén cháng shàn jiù rén, gù wú qì rén.

Therefore | sage | always/constant | good | save/rescue | people, | so | not have | abandoned | people.

The sage always preserves things, so nothing is abandoned.
This is called ancient wisdom.

> 常善救物，故无弃物。是谓袭明。
> Cháng shàn jiù wù, gù wú qì wù. Shì wèi xí míng.

Always/constant | good at | preserve value of | things/creatures, | so | not have | reject | things/creatures. |
So | speak | ancient pattern | wisdom.

▸ 袭 (xí) generally means *to attack, to raid*, but it can also mean *to follow an ancient pattern or recipe*, which is the best fit here.

So, a good person is the teacher of a bad one,
And a bad person is a lesson for a good one.

> 故，善人者不善人之师，不善人者善人之资。
> Gù, shàn rén zhě, bùshàn rén zhī shī, bù shàn rén zhě, shàn rén zhī zī.

So, | good | person | he/she | not good | person | of⇋ | teacher/example, |
Not | good | person | him/her | good | person | of⇋ | provide/assist/aid.

▸ Because only by knowing bad people can we recognize good people.

If no respect for the teacher, then no care for the lesson.

> 不贵其师，不爱其资。
> Bù guì qí shī, bù ài qí zī.

Not | valuable | his/her | teacher/example, | not | love | his/her | provide/assist/aid.

Even with wisdom there is great confusion.
This is called the essence of mystery.

虽智大迷。是谓要妙。
Suī zhì dà mí. Shì wèi yào miào.

Even though | wisdom | great | confusion. |
Is | called | essence | mystery.

28

Know the male but maintain the female.
Be a mountain stream in the world.

Be a mountain stream.
The constant De will remain,
Returning you to being a newborn.

Know the bright but maintain the dark.
Be an example in the world.

Be an example.
The constant De will not fail,
It will return you to being limitless.

Know your honor but maintain your disgrace.
Be a valley in the world.

Be a valley.
The constant De will satisfy,
Returning you to simplicity.

When the simple comes apart,
The sage uses it as a tool.

He becomes a public servant,
And great systems are not shattered.

Know the male but maintain the female.
Be a mountain stream in the world.

> 知其雄守其雌。为天下溪。
> Zhī qí xióng shǒu qí cí. Wéi tiānxià xī.

Know | his/her | male | guard | his/her | female. |
As | under heaven | mountain stream.

▶ In these opening lines, 守 (shǒu) means *guard, abide by the law, observe rules or rituals*.

Be a mountain stream.
The constant De will remain,
Returning you to being a newborn.

> 为天下溪。常德不离，复归于婴儿。
> Wéi tiānxià xī. Cháng dé bù lí, fùguī yú yīng'ér.

As | under heaven | mountain stream. |
Common | De | not | leave, |
Return | to | baby.

Know the bright but maintain the dark.
Be an example in the world.

> 知其白守其黑。为天下式。
> Zhī qí bái shǒu qí hēi. Wéi tiānxià shì.

Know | his/her | white | guard | his/her | black. |
Make | under heaven | example.

Be an example.
The constant De will not fail,
It will return you to being limitless.

> 为天下式。常德不忒，复归于无极。
> Wéi tiānxià shì. Cháng dé bú tè, fùguī yú wú jí.

As | under heaven | example. |
Common | De | not | mistake, |
Return | to | no | extreme.

Know your honor but maintain your disgrace.
Be a valley in the world.

> 知其荣守其辱。为天下谷。
> Zhī qí róng shǒu qí rǔ. Wéi tiānxià gǔ.

Know | his/her | glory | guard | his/her | humiliate. |
As | under heaven | valley.

Be a valley.
The constant De will satisfy,
Returning you to simplicity.

> 为天下谷。常德乃足，复归于朴。
> Wéi tiānxià gǔ. Cháng dé nǎi zú, fùguī yú pǔ.

Make | under heaven | valley. |
Common | De | thus | ample/abundant, |
Return | to | simple/honest.

When the simple comes apart, the sage uses it as a tool.

> 朴散则为器，圣人用之。
> Pǔ sàn zé wéi qì, shèngrén yòng zhī.

Simple/honest | scatter | then | as | instrument, | sage | uses | it.

▸ 朴 (pǔ) means both *simple* but also *an uncarved block of wood*. Try reading these two previous lines both ways.

He becomes a public servant, and great systems are not shattered.

> 则为官长，故大制不割。
> Zé wéi guānzhǎng, gù dà zhì bù gē.

Then | as | public servant, | so | large | system | not | to cut off.

▶ This last line is wonderfully ambiguous. Literally it's "so large systems are not cut off." Some have interpreted this politically, as in "the sage does not use violence to rule" or, as above, "the sage rules the state carefully and preserves it." Others read this more personally, as "when the sage cuts, things are not divided."

29

Take the world and control it?
I don't see how it can be done.

The world is a marvel,
You can't control it.
Act and you ruin it,
Grasp and you lose it.

So, creatures can lead or follow,
Can breathe shallow or deep,
Can be strong or weak,
Can be kept down or rise up.

So, the sage
Abandons overdoing, wastefulness, and pride.

Take the world and control it?
I don't see how it can be done.

> 将欲取天下而为之？吾见其不得已。
> Jiāng yù qǔ tiānxià ér wéi zhī? Wú jiàn qí bùdéyǐ.

> Will | want | take | under heaven | and | act | it? |
> I | see | his/her | not get.

The world is a marvel,
You can't control it.

> 天下神器，不可为也。
> Tiānxià shénqì, bùkě wéi yě.

> Under heaven | sacred vessel, | cannot | act | <!>.

Act and you ruin it,
Grasp and you lose it.

> 为者败之，执者失之。
> Wéi zhě bài zhī, zhí zhě shī zhī.

> Act | he/she | defeat | it, |
> Hold in hand | he/she | lose | it.

So, creatures can lead or follow,
Can breathe shallow or deep,

> 故，物或行或随，或歔或吹,
> Gù, wù huò xíng huò suí, huò xū huò chuī,

> So, | things/creatures | or | walk/advance | or | follow/submit, |
> Or | breathe quietly | or | snort/blow,

Can be strong or weak,
Can be kept down or rise up.

> 或强或羸，或挫或隳。
> Huò qiáng huò léi, huò cuò huò huī.

Or | strong | or | weak, |
Or | dampen | or | overthrow.

So, the sage
Abandons overdoing, wastefulness, and pride.

> 是以圣人去甚，去奢，去泰。
> Shìyǐ shèngrén qù shèn, qù shē, qù tài.

Therefore | sage |
Go/remove | considerable, | go/remove | extravagant, | go/remove | exalted.

30

Use Dao to assist the lords of the people,
But don't use military force,
For there will be retribution.

Where armies camp, thorns grow.
After armies leave, the harvest is poor.

The wise get results and then stop,
Not daring to take by force.

Results without bragging,
Results without boasting,
Results without arrogance,
Results only as a last resort,
Results without a show of strength.

Creatures grow strong, then age.
This is called not Dao.
Not Dao soon ends.

Use Dao to assist the lords of the people,
But don't use military force,

> 以道佐人主者，不以兵强天下，
> Yǐ dào zuǒ rén zhǔ zhě, bùyǐ bīng qiáng tiānxià,

Use | Dao | assist | people | chief/lord/master | he/she, |
Do not | soldier | force | under heaven,

For there will be retribution.

> 其事好还。
> Qí shì hào huán.

This | things/issues/problems | easily | retribution/payback.

Where armies camp, thorns grow.

> 师之所处，荆棘生焉。
> Shī zhī suǒ chù, jīngjí shēng yān.

Armies | of⇆ | where | settle/at, | thorns | birth | <!>.

After armies leave, the harvest is poor.

> 大军之后，必有凶年。
> Dà jūn zhī hòu, bì yǒu xiōng nián.

Great | army | of⇆ | after, | must | have | bad | year.

The wise get results and then stop,
Not daring to take by force.

> 善有果而已，不敢以取强。
> Shàn yǒu guǒ ér yǐ, bù gǎn yǐ qǔ qiáng.

> Good/virtue | have | result/fruit | yet | stop, |
> Not | dare | to | take | strength.

Results without bragging,
Results without boasting,

> 果而勿矜，果而勿伐，
> Guǒ ér wù jīn, guǒ ér wù fá,

> Result | yet | must not | conceited, |
> Result | yet | must not | stab/chop/attack,

Results without arrogance,
Results only as a last resort,

> 果而勿骄，果而不得已，
> Guǒ ér wù jiāo, guǒ ér bùdéyǐ,

> Result | yet | must not | haughty/spirited horse, |
> Result | yet | last resort,

Results without a show of strength.

> 果而勿强。
> Guǒ ér wù qiáng.

> Result | yet | must not | strength.

Creatures grow strong, then age.
This is called not Dao.
Not Dao soon ends.

> 物壮则老。是谓不道。不道早已。
> Wù zhuàng zé lǎo. Shì wèi bú dào. Bú dào zǎo yǐ.

Things/creatures | robust/large | then | old. |
This | says | not | Dao. |
Not | Dao | soon | stop.

▶ All creatures age and decline after reaching their prime. Laozi may be giving advice to rulers here, saying that the desire to grow strong (for example, raising an army) is often done in haste, which results in waning later and is against the unhurried nature of Dao.

31

Fine weapons are tools of misfortune.
People hate them.
So, one who has Dao does not live by them.

The nobleman usually honors the left,
But when he commands troops, he honors the right.

Weapons are tools of misfortune,
They are not the tools of a nobleman.
When using them, it's best to be restrained.

If you are victorious, don't embrace it.
If you embrace it, you enjoy killing people.
One who enjoys killing people
Can't get what they want in the world!

Good things always on the left,
Bad things always on the right.
The lieutenant general stands on the left,
The general stands on the right.
Treat it like a funeral ceremony.

Many people are killed,
Pitiful cries of sorrow,
Victory in war should be treated like a funeral ceremony.

Fine weapons are tools of misfortune.

> 夫佳兵者不祥之器。
> Fū jiā bīng zhě bùxiáng zhī qì.

So | beautiful/excellent | soldier/weapon | things | bad omen | of ⇆ | tool.

People hate them.

> 物或恶之。
> Wù huò wù zhī.

Beings | might | hate | it.

So, one who has Dao does not live by them.

> 故有道者不处。
> Gù yǒu dào zhě bù chǔ.

Therefore | have | Dao | he/she | not | reside.

The nobleman usually honors the left,
But when he commands troops, he honors the right.

> 君子居则贵左，用兵则贵右。
> Jūnzǐ jū zé guì zuǒ, yòngbīng zé guì yòu.

Gentleman | usually | method | valuable | left, |
Employs | troops | method | valuable | right.

▸ 君子 (jūnzǐ) is a nobleman, a refined gentleman, a man of high rank.

▸ Unlike in the West, Chinese culture has no bias against the left hand. An old saying is "the left eye sees wealth; the right eye sees disaster." The Chinese character for *left*, 左 (zuǒ), contains the symbol 工, meaning *work*, but the character for *right*, 右 (yòu), contains the symbol 口, meaning *mouth* and suggesting speaking or eating.

Weapons are tools of misfortune,
They are not the tools of a nobleman.

> 兵者不祥之器，非君子之器。
> Bīng zhě bùxiáng zhī qì, fēi jūnzǐ zhī qì.

Soldier/weapons | things | ominous | of⇆ | tool, |
Not | moral man | of⇆ | tool.

When using them, it's best to be restrained.

> 不得已而用之，恬淡为上。
> Bùdéyǐ ér yòng zhī, tiándàn wéi shàng.

Last resort | thus | use | it, | tranquil | as | best.

▶ 恬淡 (tiándàn): *calm, quiet, content, indifferent to fame or gain*

If you are victorious, don't embrace it.
If you embrace it, you enjoy killing people.

> 胜，而不美。而美之者，是乐杀人。
> Shèng, ér bù měi. Ér měi zhī zhě, shì lè shā rén.

Victory, | but | not | embrace. |
While | embrace | of⇆ | he/she, | is | happy | kill | people.

▶ 美 (měi) usually *beautiful*, but here, *embrace* or *glorify*

One who enjoys killing people
Can't get what they want in the world!

> 夫乐杀人者则不可以得志于天下矣。
> Fū lè shā rén zhě, zé bùkěyǐ dé zhì yú tiānxià yǐ.

So | happy | kill | people | he/she |
Then | cannot | obtain | purpose | regarding | under heaven | <!>.

Good things always on the left,
Bad things always on the right.

> 吉事尚左，凶事尚右。
> Jí shì shàng zuǒ, xiōng shì shàng yòu.

Fortunate | matters | value | left, |
Bad | matters | value | right.

The lieutenant general stands on the left,
The general stands on the right.
Treat it like a funeral ceremony.

> 偏将军居左，上将军居右。言以丧礼处之。
> Piān jiāngjūn jū zuǒ, shàng jiàngjūn jū yòu. Yán yǐ sānglǐ chǔ zhī.

Assistant | general | at | left, |
Top | general | at | right. |
Called | with | funeral ceremony | treat | it.

Many people are killed,
Pitiful cries of sorrow,
Victory in war should be treated like a funeral ceremony.

> 杀人之众，以哀悲泣之，战胜以丧礼处之。
> Shā rén zhī zhòng, yǐ āi bēi qì zhī, zhàn shèng yǐ sānglǐ chǔ zhī.

Kill | people | of ⇆ | many, |
With | pitiful | sorrow | cry | it, |
War | victory | with | funeral ceremony | treat | it.

32

Dao is forever nameless.

Even though it's simple and small,
In this world it can't be conquered!

If lords and kings could maintain it,
The ten thousand creatures would submit.
Heaven and earth would join together,
And a sweet dew would fall.

No citizens would force this,
But it would naturally be in harmony.

In the beginning, it had a name.
Having a name, men would know when to stop.
Knowing when to stop, they avoid danger.

Dao in this world is like a stream in the valley,
Flowing into a river,
Into the sea.

Dao is forever nameless.

> 道常无名。
> Dào cháng wúmíng.

Dao | frequent/common | without name.

Even though it's simple and small,
In this world it can't be conquered!

> 朴虽小，天下莫能臣也。
> Pǔ suī xiǎo, tiānxià mònéng chén yě.

Simple | even though | small, |
Under heaven | cannot | minister/official | <!>.

▶ 朴 (pǔ): as we noted in Chapter 28, this means *simple*, but also *an uncarved block of wood*. This word appears often in DDJ, reflecting Laozi's belief that nature is most powerful when in its original, unchanged, and natural form. So this could be read as "Nature in its original form is small but cannot be conquered."

▶ 臣 (chén): a *minister, official or statesman, one who controls*.

If lords and kings could maintain it,
The ten thousand creatures would submit.

> 侯王若能守之，万物将自宾。
> Hóu wáng ruò néng shǒuzhī, wànwù jiāng zì bīn.

Lord | king | if | can | keep it, |
Ten thousand things/creatures | will | oneself | submit/guest.

▶ 侯 (hóu): *the third level of Chinese nobility*, below the king and dukes

Heaven and earth would join together,
And a sweet dew would fall.

> 天地相合，以降甘露。
> Tiān dì xiàng hé, yǐ jiàng gān lù.

Heaven | earth | together | combine, |
Thus | descend | sweet | dew.

▸ In other words, the kingdom is at peace.

No citizens would force this,
But it would naturally be in harmony.

> 民莫之令，而自均。
> Mín mò zhī lìng, ér zì jūn.

Citizens | none | of⇆ | cause/command, |
Yet | natural | harmony.

In the beginning, it had a name.

> 始，制有名。
> Shǐ, zhì yǒu míng.

Start, | system | have | name.

▸ 制 (zhì): *system, order, having a social structure.* We just use "it" here.

Having a name, men would know when to stop.
Knowing when to stop, they avoid danger.

> 名亦既有，夫亦将知止。知止，所以不殆。
> Míng yì jì yǒu, fū yì jiāng zhī zhǐ. Zhī zhǐ, suǒyǐ bù dài.

Name | also | already | have, | men | also | will | know | stop. |
Know | stop, | so | no | danger.

▸ 止 (zhǐ): *stop, halt, desist, pause*

▶ Put another way: when Dao enters this world, it is named. And when it starts to act in this world, it can prevent people from excess, from "filling up."

Dao in this world is like a stream in the valley,
Flowing into a river,
Into the sea.

> 譬道之在天下，犹川谷之与江，海。
> Pì dào zhī zài tiānxià, yóu chuān gǔ zhī yǔ jiāng, hǎi.

For example | Dao | of ⇆ | at | under heaven | same | stream | valley | it, |
Flow into | river, |
Sea.

▶ 譬 (pì): *an analogy, an example, for example.* Here, we just use "like" to show that it's an analogy.

33

Know people and you are clever,
Know yourself and you have insight.

Triumph over other people and you have influence,
Triumph over yourself and you are strong.

Know you have enough and you are rich,
Be determined and you will have a strong will.

Don't lose your place, and you will endure,
Die but don't be destroyed, and you will live forever.

Know people and you are clever,
Know yourself and you have insight.

> 知人者智，自知者明。
> Zh rén zhě zhì, zì zhī zhě míng.

Know | people | he/she | intelligent/bright, |
Self | know | he/she | bright/wise.

Triumph over other people and you have influence,
Triumph over yourself and you are strong.

> 胜人者有力，自胜者强。
> Shèng rén zhě yǒu lì, zì shèng zhě qiáng.

Victory/win | people | he/she | has | power/capability/influence, |
Self | victory/win | he/she | strong.

Know you have enough and you are rich,
Be determined and you will have a strong will.

> 知足者富，强行者有志。
> Zhī zú zhě fù, qiángxíng zhě yǒu zhì.

Understand | satisfaction | he/she | abundant, |
Perseverance | he/she | has | will/aspiration.

Don't lose your place and you will endure,
Die but don't be destroyed and you will live forever.

> 不失其所者久，死而不亡者寿。
> Bù shī qí suǒ zhě jiǔ, sǐ ér bù wáng zhě shòu.

Not | lose/make mistake | his/her | place | he/she | long time, |
Die | yet | not | destroyed | he/she | old age/long life.

▶ 所 (suǒ): *place, spot, position*. Like so much else in the DDJ, this can be read personally ("don't lose your center") or socially and politically ("don't lose your position in society").

34

Great Dao is like a flood!
It can flow left and right.

The ten thousand creatures depend on it for life,
It doesn't reject them.
It completes its tasks but takes no name.

It clothes and supports the ten thousand creatures,
But is not their master.

Having no desire,
It can be called insignificant.

The ten thousand creatures return, but it is not their master,
It can be called great.

In the end it doesn't make itself great,
And so it achieves greatness.

Great Dao is like a flood!
It can flow left and right.

> 大道泛兮，其可左右。
> Dà dào fàn xī, qí kě zuǒ yòu.

Great/big | Dao | extensive/flood | <!>, |
It | can | left | right.

▸ Here 大道 (dà dào) means *great Dao*, not *highest social order* as it did in Chapter 18.

▸ To flow left and right is to flow everywhere.

The ten thousand creatures depend on it for life,
It doesn't reject them.

> 万物恃之而生，而不辞。
> Wànwù shì zhī ér shēng, ér bù cí.

Ten thousand things/creatures | rely on | it | then | birth/life, |
Then | not | shirk.

It completes its tasks but takes no name.

> 功成不名有。
> Gōng chéng bù míng yǒu.

Achieve | complete | not | name | take.

It clothes and supports the ten thousand creatures,
But is not their master.

> 衣养万物，而不为主。
> Yī yǎng wànwù, ér bù wéi zhǔ.

Clothes/covers | support | ten thousand things/creatures, |

Yet | not | as | master.

Having no desire,
It can be called insignificant.

> 常无欲，可名于小。
> Cháng wú yù, kě míng yú xiǎo.

Often | not have | desire, |
Can | name | be | small.

The ten thousand creatures return, but it is not their master,

> 万物归焉，而不为主。
> Wànwù guī yān, ér bù wéi zhǔ.

Ten thousand things/creatures | return | <!>, |
Yet | not | as | master.

It can be called great.
In the end it doesn't make itself great,

> 可名为大。以其终不自为大，
> Kě míng wéi dà. Yǐ qí zhōng bù zì wéi dà,

Can | name | as | large. |
With | he/she/it | in the end | not | him/her/itself | as | large,

And so it achieves greatness.

> 故能成其大。
> Gù néng chéng qí dà.

Thus | can | achieve | he/she/it | large/great.

▶ 其 (qí) is a general pronoun. In these last three lines we read 其 as *it*, talking about Dao. But some read 其 as *him*, interpreting these lines as talking about the sage.

35

Holding the great image in its hands,
The whole world comes to it.

Come to it without hurting each other,
There is safety and peace.

Music and good food make guests stay,
But Dao's words come out weak and flavorless!

Look for it, you can't see it,
Listen for it, you can't hear it,
Use it, you can't exhaust it.

Holding the great image in its hands,
The whole world comes to it.

> 执大象，天下往。
> Zhí dà xiàng, tiānxià wǎng.

Hold | large/great | image, |
Under heaven | towards.

▶ 象 (xiàng): *elephant* or *carved image*

▶ There's no pronoun in any of the first three lines, so it's tricky to say who, or what, is holding the image. Some translate this as "his hands," meaning the sage, or "your hands." But based on the rest of the chapter, we prefer "it," meaning the Dao. You could also eliminate the pronouns entirely and read this as "Grasping the great image, the whole world comes."

Come to it without hurting each other,
There is safety and peace.

> 往而不害，安平大。
> Wǎng ér bùhài, ānpíng dà.

Towards | but | don't hurt others, |
Safe/quiet/calm | large/great.

Music and good food make guests stay,

> 乐与饵，过客止。
> Yuè yǔ ěr, guò kè zhǐ.

Music | and | bait/enticement, | passing | guests | stop/desist.

But Dao's words come out weak and flavorless!

> 道之出口，淡乎其无味，
> Dào zhī chū kǒu, dàn hū qí wúwèi.

Dao | of⇆ | go out | mouth, | weak/watery | <!> | it | not has | taste.

Look for it, you can't see it,
Listen for it, you can't hear it,

> 视之不足见，听之不足闻，
> Shì zhī bùzú jiàn, tīng zhī bùzú wén,

Look | it | insufficient/can't | see, |
Listen | it | insufficient/can't | hear,

Use it, you can't exhaust it.

> 用之，不足既。
> Yòng zhī, bùzú jì.

Use | it, | insufficient/can't | satiated.

▶ 既 (jì): *finish up*, a man turning away after finishing eating

36

When you want to draw something in,
You must first stretch it out.

When you want to weaken something,
You must first make it strong.

When you want to abandon something,
You must first promote it.

When you want to seize something,
You must first give it something.

This is subtle wisdom.

Soft and weak conquers hard and strong,
Fish can't escape from deep waters.

The sharp tools of the nation
Can't be shown to the people.

When you want to draw something in,
You must first stretch it out.

> 将欲歙之，必固张之。
> Jiāng yù xī zhī, bì gù zhāng zhī.

Would | want | suck/inhale | it, |
Surely | no doubt | stretch | it.

▶ 歙 (xī): *suck* or *inhale*

When you want to weaken something,
You must first make it strong.

> 将欲弱之，必固强之。
> Jiāng yù ruò zhī, bì gù qiáng zhī.

Would | want | weak/delicate | it, |
Surely | no doubt | strong | it.

When you want to abandon something,
You must first promote it.

> 将欲废之，必固兴之。
> Jiāng yù fèi zhī, bì gù xìng zhī.

Would | want | abandon/discard | it, |
Surely | no doubt | prosper | it.

When you want to seize something,
You must first give it something.

> 将欲夺之，必固与之。
> Jiāng yù duó zhī, bì gù yǔ zhī.

Would | want | take by force | it, |
Surely | no doubt | give | it.

This is subtle wisdom.

> 是谓微明。
> Shì wèi wēi míng.

Is | called | subtle | wisdom.

Soft and weak conquers hard and strong,
Fish can't escape from deep waters.

> 柔弱胜刚强，鱼不可脱于渊。
> Róu ruò shèng gāng qiáng, yú bùkě tuō yú yuān.

Soft | weak | win | hard | strong, |
Fish | cannot | escape | of | gulf/abyss.

The sharp tools of the nation
Can't be shown to the people.

> 国之利器不可以示人。
> Guó zhī lì qì bùkě yǐ shì rén.

Nation | of ⇆ | sharp | instrument |
Cannot | with | show | people.

37

Dao does nothing,
Yet nothing is left undone.

If lords and kings could grasp this,
The ten thousand creatures would transform themselves.

If transformation leads to desire,
I will suppress it by using nameless simplicity.

Nameless simplicity eliminates desire.

Without desire all is peaceful,
And the world settles itself.

Dao does nothing,
Yet nothing is left undone.

> 道常无为，而无不为。
> Dào cháng wúwéi, ér wú bù wéi.

Dao | eternally | empty action, |
Yet | nothing | not | doing.

▶ A key idea in the DDJ is 为无为 (wéiwúwéi), *doing without doing.* This is not being lazy or apathetic, but acting without interfering and without care for the result. Here in the first line, 无为 (wúwéi) means *empty action* or *not doing*. In the second, a 不 (bù) is inserted, another negative, giving 无不为 (wúbùwéi), literally *without not doing*.

If lords and kings could grasp this,
The ten thousand creatures would transform themselves.

> 侯王若能守之，万物将自化。
> Hóu wáng ruò néng shǒu zhī, wànwù jiāng zì huà.

Lord | king | if | can | observe/defend | it, |
Ten thousand things/creatures | will | oneself | transform.

If transformation leads to desire,
I will suppress it by using nameless simplicity.

> 化而欲作，吾将镇之以无名之朴。
> Huà ér yù zuò, wú jiāng zhèn zhī yǐ wúmíng zhī pǔ.

Transform | like | desire | arise/grow, |
I | will | suppress | it | with | nameless | of 与 | simple/rough.

▶ Key to this chapter's meaning is 朴 (pǔ), *simple,* but also *an uncarved block of wood.* One can neutralize desire by returning to one's original state of unmodified simplicity.

Nameless simplicity eliminates desire.

> 无名之朴夫亦将无欲。
> Wúmíng zhī pǔ fū yì jiāng wú yù.

No name | of⇆ | simple/rough | thus | also | would | no | desire.

Without desire all is peaceful,
And the world settles itself.

> 不欲以静，天下将自定。
> Bú yù yǐ jìng, tiānxià jiāng zì dìng.

Without | desire | then | quiet, |
Under heaven | about to | oneself | settle/fix.

Part 2: De Jing

德经

38

One with high De has no De, and so truly has De.
One with low De never loses De, and so truly has no De.

One with high De does nothing and has no selfish motives.
One with low De acts and has selfish motives.
A kind person acts and has no selfish motives.
A moral person acts and has selfish motives.

A well-mannered person acts but no one responds,
They roll up their sleeves and force others to respond.

Lose Dao and you have De,
Lose De and you have kindness,
Lose kindness and you have morality.
Lose morality and you have good behavior.

Good behavior looks like loyalty and honesty,
But it's the beginning of confusion.

People have crazy preconceptions about Dao,
That's the beginning of foolishness.

So, the sage
Lives by the substantial, not the weak,
Lives by the truth, not crazy ideas.
He leaves that and choose this.

One with high De has no De, and so truly has De.

> 上德不德，是以有德。
> Shàng dé bù dé, shìyǐ yǒu dé.

High | De | not | De, | therefore | has | De.

▶ These two lines can be read many ways. The most literal and minimal first line is "The best De is not De, so it has De." But since De is all about a person's actions in harmony with Dao (see definition of Dé in the glossary), these lines probably are best understood as relating to people, not just to De itself. So we add the pronoun "one" and translate these lines as they relate to a personal way of life.

One with low De never loses De, and so truly has no De.

> 下德不失德，是以无德。
> Xià dé bù shī dé, shìyǐ wú dé.

Low | De | not | lose | De, | therefore | without | De.

▶ Someone with little or no De is afraid to lose sight of their De, thus they don't really have De.

One with high De does nothing and has no selfish motives.
One with low De acts and has selfish motives.
A kind person acts and has no selfish motives.
A moral person acts and has selfish motives.

> 上德无为而无以为。下德为之而有以为。
> 上仁为之而无以为。上义为之而有以为。
> Shàng dé wúwéi ér wú yǐwéi. Xià dé wéi zhī ér yǒu yǐwéi.
> Shàng rén wéi zhī ér wú yǐwéi. Shàng yì wéi zhī ér yǒu yǐwéi.

High | De | empty action | therefore | without | deliberately act. |

Low | De | act | it | therefore | have | deliberately act. |
High | kindness | act | it | therefore | not have | deliberately act. |
High | righteousness | act | it | therefore | have | deliberately act.

▸ First Laozi shows us the the virtues of having De, and then three ways of not having it, including the third where he tells us that acting kindly is actually misguided when compared with the powerful non-action of De.

▸ 以为 (yǐwéi) here means *selfish motive*. It literally means *think*, that is, to think of yourself, to act with calculation about the effect of the results. It's the opposite of 为无为 (wéi wú wéi), doing without doing.

A well-mannered person acts but no one responds,
They roll up their sleeves and force others to respond.

> 上礼为之而莫之应则，攘臂而扔之。
> Shàng lǐ wéi zhī ér mò zhī yìng zé, rǎng bì ér rēng zhī.

High | manners | act | of⇆ | but | cannot | of⇆ | respond | <!>, |
Stretch out | arm | then | throw | it.

▸ Someone with 上礼 (shàng lǐ) has good manners and courtesy, is well behaved.

Lose Dao and you have De,
Lose De and you have kindness,

> 故失道而后德，失德而后仁，
> Gù shī dào ér hòu dé, shī dé ér hòu rén,

So | lose | Dao | then | later | De, |
Lose | De | then | later | kindness,

Lose kindness and you have morality,
Lose morality and you have good behavior.

> 失仁而后义，失义而后礼。
> Shī rén ér hòu yì, shī yì ér hòu lǐ.

Lose | kindness | then | later | righteousness, |
Lose | righteousness | then | later | social customs.

Good behavior looks like loyalty and honesty,
But it's the beginning of confusion.

> 夫礼者忠信之薄，而乱之首。
> Fū lǐ zhě zhōng xìn zhī báo, ér luàn zhī shǒu.

So | social customs | he/she | loyalty | true | of 之 | weak/flimsy, |
Then | confusion/chaos | of 之 | first.

People have crazy preconceptions about Dao,
That's the beginning of foolishness.

> 前识者道之华，而愚之始。
> Qiánshì zhě dào zhī huá, ér yú zhī shǐ.

Prior knowledge | he/she | Dao | of 之 | flashy, |
Then | stupid | of 之 | begin.

▶ 前识 (qiánshì): *prior knowledge*, referring here to people with preconceived and misguided ideas about Dao.

▶ 华 (huá) has several meanings including *flower, splendid, ornate* or *flashy*. Here it likely means *flashy* or *crazy ideas*, in the sense of "something that looks pretty but is not real." The word appears again in the next line, where it's contrasted with 实 (shí) which means *real, solid, true*.

So, the sage
Lives by the substantial, not the weak,

> 是以大丈夫处其厚不居其薄,
> Shìyǐ dàzhàngfū chǔ qí hòu bù jū qí bó,

Therefore | great men |
Reside | his | thick/deep/rich, | not | sit | his | thin/weak,

Lives by the truth, not crazy ideas.

> 处其实,不居其华。
> Chǔ qí shí, bù jū qí huá.

Reside | its | solid/fruit, | not | sit | its | flashy.

He leaves that and choose this.

> 故去彼取此。
> Gù qù bǐ qǔ cǐ.

So | give up | that | take | this.

39

Ancients who have attained oneness:
The sky attained oneness and became clear.
Earth attained oneness and became peaceful,
The gods attained oneness and became divine,
The valley attained oneness and became full,
The ten thousand creatures attained oneness and flourished,
Lords and kings attained oneness and became leaders.

In other words,
If the sky were not clear, I'm afraid it would break apart.
If earth were not peaceful, I'm afraid it would erupt.
If the gods were not wise, I'm afraid they would disappear.
If the valley were not full, I'm afraid it would be used up.
If the ten thousand creatures were not growing, I'm afraid they would be wiped out.
If lords and kings were not high up, I'm afraid they would fall.

High rank has its origin in low value,
The high has its foundation in the low.
Thus lords and kings call themselves orphaned, lonely, and hungry.
Isn't this because the root of high rank is low value?
Isn't it?

Many honors is the same as no honor.

Don't desire to be precious like jade,
Be common like rock.

Ancients who have attained oneness:
The sky attained oneness and became clear.

> 昔之得一者：天得一以清。
> Xī zhī dé yī zhě: Tiān dé yī yǐ qīng.

Past | of⇆ | obtain | one | it: |
Heaven | obtain | one | therefore | clear.

▶ 天 (tiān): *sky* or *heaven*, depending on context

Earth attained oneness and became peaceful,
The gods attained oneness and became divine,

> 地得一以宁，神得一以灵，
> Dì dé yī yǐ níng, shén dé yī yǐ líng,

Earth | obtain | one | therefore | serene, |
God | obtain | one | therefore | godlike/wise,

The valley attained oneness and became full,
The ten thousand creatures attained oneness and flourished,

> 谷得一以盈，万物得一以生，
> Gǔ dé yī yǐ yíng, wànwù dé yī yǐ shēng,

Valley | obtain | one | therefore | full, |
Ten thousand things/creatures | obtain | one | therefore | grow/flourish,

Lords and kings attained oneness and became leaders.

> 侯王得一以为天下贞。
> Hóu wáng dé yī yǐ wéi tiānxià zhēn.

Lords | kings | obtain | one | therefore | as | under heaven | virtuous/leader.

In other words,
If the sky were not clear, I'm afraid it would break apart.

> 其致之，天无以清，将恐裂。
> Qí zhì zhī, tiān wú yǐ qīng, jiāng kǒng liè.

It | to | it, |
Sky/heaven | not | with | clear, | will | fear | crack/split.

▶ 其致之 (qí zhì zhī): *in other words*

If earth were not peaceful, I'm afraid it would erupt.

> 地无以宁，将恐发。
> Dì wú yǐ níng, jiāng kǒng fā.

Earth | not have | with | serene, | will | fear | issue/send out.

If the gods were not wise, I'm afraid they would disappear.

> 神无以灵，将恐歇。
> Shén wú yǐ líng, jiāng kǒng xiē.

Spirit | not have | with | soul, | will | fear | disappear.

If the valley were not full, I'm afraid it would be used up.

> 谷无以盈，将恐竭。
> Gǔ wú yǐ yíng, jiāng kǒng jié.

Valley | not have | with | full, | will | fear | exhaust.

If the ten thousand creatures were not growing, I'm afraid they would be wiped out.

> 万物无以生，将恐灭。
> Wànwù wú yǐ shēng, jiāng kǒng miè.

Ten thousand things/creatures | not | with | grow/flourish, | will | fear | wipe out.

If lords and kings were not high up, I'm afraid they would fall.

> 侯王无以贵高，将恐蹶。
> Hóu wáng wú yǐ guì gāo, jiāngkǒng jué.

Lords | kings | not | with | valuable | high, | will fear | fall down.

▶ 贵高 (guì gāo): literally, *expensive and lofty*

High rank has its origin in low value,
The high has its foundation in the low.

> 故贵以贱为本，高以下为基。
> Gù guì yǐ jiàn wéi běn, gāo yǐ xià wèi jī.

So | high/noble/costly | with | cheap | as | root/origin, |
High | with | low | as | foundation.

Thus lords and kings call themselves orphaned, lonely, and hungry.

> 是以侯王自称孤、寡、不谷。
> Shìyǐ hóu wáng zìchēng gū, guǎ, bù gǔ.

Therefore | lords | kings | self-proclaimed | alone, | widowed, | not | valley/grain.

Isn't this because the root of high rank is low value?
Isn't it?

> 此非以贱为本耶？非乎？
> Cǐ fēi yǐ jiàn wéi běn yé? Fēi hū?

This | not | with | lowly | as | root | <!>? |
Not | <!>?

Many honors is the same as no honor.

> 故致数誉无誉。
> Gù zhì shù yù wú yù.

So | cause | several | fame | not | fame.

Don't desire to be precious like jade,
Be common like rock.

> 不欲琭琭如玉，珞珞如石。
> Bú yù lùlù rú yù, luòluò rú shí.

Not | desire | beautiful like jade | like | jade, |
Hard like rock | like | stone.

40

The motion of Dao is to return.
The function of Dao is to weaken.

The ten thousand creatures of the world are born from being;
Being is born from non-being.

The motion of Dao is to return.
The function of Dao is to weaken.

> 反者道之动。弱者道之用。
> Fǎn zhě dào zhī dòng. Ruòzhě dào zhī yòng.

Cycle back and forth | it | Dao | of⇆ | act/move/touch. | Weak | it | Dao | of⇆ | use.

The ten thousand creatures of the world are born from being;
Being is born from non-being.

> 天下万物生于有。有生于无。
> Tiānxià wànwù shēng yú yǒu. Yǒu shēng yú wú.

Under heaven | ten thousand things/creatures | born | of | existence. | Existence | born | of | absence.

▶ 有 (yǒu) commonly means *have*, but here, it means *existence* or *beingness*. It's the opposite of 无 (wú), *not-being*.

41

The highest student hears Dao, and practices it diligently.
The middle student hears Dao, but is unsure.
The lowest student hears Dao, and laughs out loud.
Without laughter, there's no Dao.

So, it is said:
The brightest Dao seems like darkness,
The boldest Dao seems like retreating,
The smoothest Dao seems to be knotted,
The highest De seems like a valley,

The whitest things seem muddy,
The broadest De seems incomplete,
The newest De seems slow,
The purest things seem murky,
The squarest things have no corners,
The greatest tools are completed last,
The greatest tones are inaudible,
The greatest images have no form,

Dao is hidden and has no name.

So, only Dao is good at giving and accomplishing.

The highest student hears Dao, and practices it diligently.

> 上士闻道，勤而行之。
> Shàng shì wén dào, qín ér xíng zhī.

Top | scholar | hears | Dao, | industrious | then | carry out | it.

The middle student hears Dao, but is unsure.

> 中士闻道，若存若亡。
> Zhōng shì wén dào, ruò cún ruò wáng.

Middle | scholar | hears | Dao, | seem | keep/live | seem | lose/die.

▶ 若存若亡 (ruò cún ruò wáng): *appears to keep, appears to lose*, that is, the student's understanding of Dao seems to come and go.

The lowest student hears Dao, and laughs out loud.

> 下士闻道，大笑之。
> Xià shì wén dào, dà xiào zhī.

Low | scholar | hears | Dao, | big | laugh/smile | it.

▶ Highest may not be better than lowest! The rest of this chapter is all about contradictions. So, perhaps the lowest student, by laughing, has the right idea.

Without laughter, there's no Dao.

> 不笑，不足以为道。
> Bú xiào, bùzú yǐ wéi dào.

Not | laugh/smile, | insufficient | so | as | Dao.

So, it is said:

> 故建言有之：
> Gù jiàn yán yǒu zhī:

So | establish | speak | have | it:

The brightest Dao seems like darkness,
The boldest Dao seems like retreating,
The smoothest Dao seems to be knotted,
The highest De seems like a valley,

> 明道若昧，进道若退，夷道若纇，上德若谷，
> Míng dào ruò mèi, jìn dào ruò tuì, yí dào ruò lèi, shàng dé ruò gǔ,

Bright | Dao | same as | dark, |
Advance | Dao | same as | retreat, |
Flat | Dao | same as | bumpy/rugged, |
Top | De | same as | valley,

The whitest things seem muddy,
The broadest De seems incomplete,
The newest De seems slow,

> 太白若辱，广德若不足，建德若偷，
> Tài bái ruò rǔ, guǎng dé ruò bù zú, jiàn dé ruò tōu,

Very | bright/white | same as | dirt/filth, |
Broad | De | same as | not | attain, |
Newly established | De | same as | lazy/drawn out/acting slowly,

▶ In the last line, newly established processes may appear to be slow and without purpose, but they are slowly creating.

The purest things seem murky,
The squarest things have no corners,

The greatest tools are completed last,

> 质真若渝，大方无隅，大器晚成，
> Zhì zhēn ruò yú, dà fāng wú yú, dà qì wǎn chéng,

Substance | real | same as | muddy/turbid, |
Great | square shape | not have | corner/remote place, |
Great | instrument | late | complete,

▶ Chinese coins are round on the outside but have square holes.

▶ 大器晚成 (dà qì wǎn chéng): a Chinese idiom, roughly equivalent to "it takes a long time to make a great pot," that is, great things mature slowly.

The greatest tones are inaudible,
The greatest images have no form,
Dao is hidden and has no name.

> 大音希声，大象无形，道隐无名。
> Dà yīn xī shēng, dà xiàng wú xíng, dào yǐn wú míng.

Great | tone | rare/sparse | sound, |
Great | image | not have | form, |
Dao | hidden | not has | name.

So, only Dao is good at giving and accomplishing.

> 夫唯道善贷且成。
> Fū wéi dào shàn dài qiě chéng.

So | only | Dao | good | bestow | and/further | become/succeed.

42

Dao gives birth to one,
One gives birth to two,
Two gives birth to three,
Three gives birth to the ten thousand creatures.

The ten thousand creatures carry Yin and embrace Yang,
Flowing together in harmony.

People hate being orphaned, lonely, and hungry,
Yet this is what kings and lords call themselves.

So, creatures
Sometimes weaken but then gain strength,
Sometimes strengthen but then grow weak.

I teach what others have taught.
Hoodlums don't die a natural death.
This is the basis of my teaching.

Dao gives birth to one,
One gives birth to two,
Two gives birth to three,
Three gives birth to the ten thousand creatures.

> 道生一，一生二，二生三，三生万物。
> Dào shēng yī, yī shēng èr, èr shēng sān, sān shēng wànwù.

Dao | born | one, |
One | born | two, |
Two | born | three, |
Three | born | ten thousand things/creatures.

The ten thousand creatures carry Yin and embrace Yang,
Flowing together in harmony.

> 万物负阴而抱阳，冲气以为和。
> Wànwù fù yīn ér bào yáng, chōng qì yǐ wéi hé.

Ten thousand things/creatures | carry/burden | yin | and | enfold | yang, |
Conflict | *qi* | so | become | harmony.

People hate being orphaned, lonely, and hungry,
Yet this is what kings and lords call themselves.

> 人之所恶唯孤、寡、不谷，而王公以为称。
> Rén zhī suǒ wù wéi gū, guǎ, bùgǔ, ér wáng gōng yǐ wéi chēng.

People | of ⇆ | what | dislike/hate | only | alone, | widowed, | worthless/unhappy/hungry, |
But | king | lord | use | as | called.

▶ 寡 (guǎ) and 不谷 (bùgǔ) don't just mean *orphan* and *lonely*, they are also self-deprecating terms used by royalty to describe themselves.

So, creatures
Sometimes weaken but then gain strength,
Sometimes strengthen but then grow weak.

> 故物或损之而益，或益之而损。
> Gù wù huò sǔn zhī ér yì, huò yì zhī ér sǔn.

So | things/creatures | or | damage | of⇆ | then | benefit, |
Or | benefit | of⇆ | then | damage.

I teach what others have taught.

> 人之所教我亦教之。
> Rén zhī suǒ jiào wǒ yì jiào zhī.

People | of⇆ | what | teach | I | also | teach | it.

Hoodlums don't die a natural death.

> 强梁者不得其死。
> Qiángliáng zhě bù dé qí sǐ.

Ruffian/bully | he/she | not | get | their | death.

This is the basis of my teaching.

> 吾将以为教父。
> Wú jiāng yǐ wéi jiào fù.

I | will/would | use | as | teaching | father/principle.

43

The softest things in the world
Overrun the hardest things.

The formless enters where there is no gap.

And so I know the benefits of not doing.

Teaching without words,
The benefit of doing nothing,
Few in the world can match this.

The softest things in the world
Overrun the hardest things.

> 天下之至柔驰骋天下之至坚。
> Tiānxià zhī zhì róu chíchěng tiānxià zhī zhì jiān.

Under heaven | of 之 | extremely | soft |
Horse gallop | under heaven | of 之 | extremely | hard.

The formless enters where there is no gap,
And so I know the benefits of not doing.

> 无有入无间，吾是以知无为之有益。
> Wú yǒu rù wú jiàn, wú shìyǐ zhī wúwéi zhī yǒu yì.

Nonexistence | have | enter | none | interval/gap, |
I | therefore | know | empty action | of 之 | have | benefit.

Teaching without words,
The benefit of doing nothing,
Few in the world can match this.

> 不言之教，无为之益，天下希及之。
> Bù yán zhī jiào, wúwéi zhī yì, tiānxià xī jí zhī.

Not have | words | of 之 | teach, |
Empty action | of 之 | benefit, |
Under heaven | rare/sparse | catch up/match | it.

44

Fame or life: which do you prefer?
Life or property: which is more precious?
Gain or loss: which is more harmful?

Great desire brings great cost.
Much gathering brings much loss.

Know when you have enough, there's no disgrace.
Know when you have to stop, there's no danger.

And so you can live a long time.

Fame or life: which do you prefer?
Life or property: which is more precious?
Gain or loss: which is more harmful?

> 名与身孰亲？身与货孰多？得与亡孰病？
> Míng yǔ shēn shú qīn? Shēn yǔ huò shú duō? Dé yǔ wáng shú bìng?

Fame | versus | life | which | prefer? |
Life | versus | goods | which | more? |
Gain/fame | versus | death/loss | which | harmful?

▶ 与 (yǔ): *versus*, used three times here. "Or" reads better in English.

Great desire brings great cost,
Much gathering brings much loss.

> 是故甚爱必大费，多藏必厚亡。
> Shì gù shèn ài bì dà fèi, duō cáng bì hòu wáng.

This | thus | great | love | surely | great | expense, |
Much | hoard/stash | surely | much | loss.

▶ 爱 (ài): *love* or *desire*

▶ 藏 (cáng): *hoarding*, collecting or gathering to an excessive degree

Know when you have enough, there's no disgrace.
Know when you have to stop, there's no danger.
And so you can live a long time.

> 知足，不辱。知止，不殆。可以长久。
> Zhī zú, bù rǔ. Zhī zhǐ, bú dài. Kěyǐ chángjiǔ.

Know | enough | not | humiliate. |
Know | stop | not | dangerous. |
Can | long time.

45

Great achievement can appear incomplete,
Use it, it won't fail.

Great fullness can appear empty,
Use it, it won't run dry.

Great straightness can appear bent.
Great skill can appear clumsy.
Great eloquence can sound like stammering.

Movement can conquer cold,
Stillness can conquer heat.

Serenity keeps the world in order.

Great achievement can appear incomplete,
Use it, it won't fail.

> 大成若缺，其用不弊。
> Dà chéng ruò quē, qí yòng bù bì.

Great | complete/finish | seems | deficit, |
Its | effect/function | not | harm/disadvantage.

Great fullness can appear empty,
Use it, it won't run dry.

> 大盈若冲，其用不穷。
> Dà yíng ruò chōng, qí yòng bù qióng.

Great | fill | seems | pour out, |
Its | effect/function | not | end/limit.

Great straightness can appear bent.
Great skill can appear clumsy.
Great eloquence can sound like stammering.

> 大直若屈，大巧若拙，大辩若讷。
> Dà zhí ruò qū, dà qiǎo ruò zhuō, dà biàn ruò nè.

Great | straight | seems | bend, |
Great | skill | seems | clumsy, |
Great | argue | seems | stammer/mumble.

Movement can conquer cold,
Stillness can conquer heat.

> 躁胜寒，静胜热。
> Zào shèng hán, jìng shèng rè.

Tense/excited | succeed/better than | cold, |
Quiet | succeed/better than | hot.

▶ 躁 (zào): *restless, tense, excited, impatient*

Serenity keeps the world in order.

> 清静为天下正。
> Qīngjìng wéi tiānxià zhèng.

Calm/not disturb | make | under heaven | straight.

46

When the world has Dao,
Riding horses work in the fields.

When the world has no Dao,
War horses give birth in the countryside.

No crime is greater than the feeling of desire.
No misfortune is greater than not knowing when enough is enough.
No fault is greater than wanting more and more.

So, know when enough is enough.
There is always enough!

When the world has Dao,
Riding horses work in the fields.

> 天下有道，却走马以粪。
> Tiānxià yǒu dào, què zǒumǎ yǐ fèn.

Under heaven | have | Dao, |
Recede/go back | riding horse | used for | manure.

▸ 粪 (fèn): *manure*. The appearance of horse manure in a field is an indicator that a horse has been used for tilling (pulling a plow). The horse is used for working the fields instead of in war, and the manure is just a byproduct.

When the world has no Dao,
War horses give birth in the countryside.

> 天下无道，戎马生于郊。
> Tiānxià wú dào, róng mǎ shēng yú jiāo.

Under heaven | without | Dao, |
Military | horse | give birth | at | outskirts.

▸ When horses are in short supply during war, even mares are pressed into service.

No crime is greater than the feeling of desire.

> 罪莫大於可欲。
> Zuì mò dà yú kě yù.

Crime/fault/error | not | great | of | want | desire.

No misfortune is greater than not knowing when enough is enough.
No fault is greater than wanting more and more.

> 祸莫大于不知足。咎莫大于欲得。
> **Huò mò dà yú bùzhīzú. Jiù mò dà yú yù dé.**

Scourge | not | great | of | not know enough. |
Fault | not | great | of | want | get.

So, know when enough is enough.
There is always enough!

> 故知足之足。常足矣。
> **Gù zhī zú zhī zú. Cháng zú yǐ.**

So, | know | enough | of⇆ | enough. |
Frequent | enough | <!>.

▶ 足 (zú): *enough, sufficient, being satisfied with what you've got*

47

Without going out the door
You can still understand the world.

Without looking out the window
You can still know the Dao of heaven.

The further you go,
The less you know.

So, the sage doesn't travel, yet knows.
Doesn't show off, yet is famous.
Doesn't act, yet accomplishes.

Without going out the door
You can still understand the world.

> 不出户知天下。
> Bù chū hù zhī tiānxià.

Not | go out | door |
Understand | under heaven.

Without looking out the window
You can still know the Dao of heaven.

> 不窥牖见天道。
> Bù kuī yǒu jiàn tiān dào.

Not | peek | window |
See | heaven | Dao.

The further you go,
The less you know.

> 其出弥远，其知弥少。
> Qí chū mí yuǎn, qí zhī mí shǎo.

<imperative> | go out | more | far off, |
<imperative> | know | more | less.

So, the sage doesn't travel, yet knows.

> 是以圣人不行，而知。
> Shìyǐ shèngrén bù xíng, ér zhī.

Therefore | sage | not | walk | yet | know.

Doesn't show off, yet is famous.
Doesn't act, yet accomplishes.

> 不见，而名。不为，而成。
> Bù jiàn, ér míng. Bù wéi, ér chéng.

Not | see/show, | yet | name/fame. |
Not | do, | yet | complete.

▸ 名 (míng) means *name*, but also *fame* or *reputation*. In modern Chinese, the word for famous is 有名 (yǒu míng), literally, *has name*.

48

For those who study, more every day.
For those who practice Dao, less every day.

Less and less,
Until you arrive at doing nothing.

Do nothing, and nothing is left undone.
To conquer the world, just do nothing.

If you must do things,
You can't conquer the world.

For those who study, more every day.

> 为学者，日益。
> Wéi xué zhě, rì yì.

To do | study | he/she, | day/daily | profit/increase.

For those who practice Dao, less every day.

> 为道者，日损。
> Wéi dào zhě, rì sǔn.

To do | Dao | he/she,| day/daily | diminish/decrease.

▶ Contrasting those who accumulate knowledge with those who study Dao.

Less and less, until you arrive at doing nothing.

> 损之又损，以至於无为。
> Sǔn zhī yòu sǔn, yǐzhìyú wúwéi.

Diminish | of⇆ | and | diminish, | So that | empty action.

Do nothing, and nothing is left undone.

> 无为，而无不为。
> Wúwéi, ér wú bù wéi.

Empty action, | yet | without | no | action.

To conquer the world, just do nothing.

> 取天下，常以无事。
> Qǔ tiānxià, cháng yǐ wú shì.

Take/get | under heaven, | always | with | no | things.

▶ Note that the end of this line is 无事 (wú shì) meaning *no things, no tasks*. This is different from 无为 (wúwéi) which means *empty action, non-action*. In other words, a great leader avoids micromanaging!

If you must do things,
You can't conquer the world.

> 及其有事，不足以取天下。
> Jí qí yǒu shì, bùzúyǐ qǔ tiānxià.

And | it | has | things, |
Not enough | get | under heaven.

49

The sage doesn't maintain his own heart,
So the common peoples' hearts become his heart.

If someone is good to me, I am good to him,
If someone is not good to me, I am still good to him,
Because De is good.

If someone is honest with me, I am honest with them,
If someone is not honest with me, I am still honest with him,
Because De is honesty.

The sage lives in the world, draws it all in,
And lets all their hearts become simple and honest.

The common people all focus on what they hear and see.
The sage has restored them to being like children.

The sage doesn't maintain his own heart,
So the common peoples' hearts become his heart.

> 圣人无常心，以百姓心为心。
> Shèngrén wú cháng xīn, yǐ bǎixìng xīn wéi xīn.

Sage | not | constant | heart/mind, |
With/use | hundred families | heart | as | heart.

If someone is good to me, I am good to him,
If someone is not good to me, I am still good to him,
Because De is good.

> 善者，吾善之，不善者，吾亦善之，德善。
> Shàn zhě, wú shàn zhī, bú shàn zhě, wú yì shàn zhī, dé shàn.

Good | he/she, | I | good | he/she, |
Not | good | he/she, | I | also | good | he/she, |
De | good.

If someone is honest with me, I am honest with them,
If someone is not honest with me, I am still honest with him,
Because De is honesty.

> 信者，吾信之，不信者，吾亦信之，德信。
> Xìn zhě, wú xìn zhī, bú xìn zhě, wú yì xìn zhī, dé xìn.

Truth | he/she, | I | truth | he/she, |
Not | truth | he/she, | I | also | truth | he/she, |
De | truth.

The sage lives in the world, draws it all in,
And lets all their hearts become simple and honest.

> 圣人在天下，歙歙为天下，浑其心。
> Shèngrén zài tiānxià, xī xī wèi tiānxià, hún qí xīn.

Sage | in | under heaven, | suck/inhale | suck/inhale | for | under heaven, |
Natural/simple | its | heart.

▶ 浑 (hún) in modern Chinese means *muddy* or *turbid*, but it has an older meaning of *simple, natural, unsophisticated*.

The common people all focus on what they hear and see.
The sage has restored them to being like children.

> 百姓皆注其耳目。圣人皆孩之。
> Bǎixìng jiē zhù qí ěr mù. Shèngrén jiē hái zhī.

Hundred families | all | pay attention to | their | ears | eyes. |
Sage | all | make like children | them.

▶ A similar thought to Chapter 12, where the sage encourages people to live simply and focus on the things in front of them, and not be distracted by foolish thoughts.

50

From beginning life to entering death,
Followers of life are three in ten,
Followers of death are three in ten,
Those who drift towards their places of death, three in ten.

Why?
Because they live for life's sensations.

It's said that one who cares intensely for life
Can travel the land and not meet rhinos or tigers,
Can enter battle without shield or sword.

The rhino has no place to thrust its horn,
The tiger has no place to use its claws,
The soldier's blade has no place to enter.

Why?
Because in him there is no place for death.

From beginning life to entering death,
Followers of life are three in ten,

> 出生入死，生之徒，十有三，
> Chūshēng rù sǐ, shēng zhī tú, shí yǒu sān,

Born (enter life) | enter | death, |
Life | of 的 | disciple, | 10 | has | 3,

Followers of death are three in ten,

> 死之徒十有三，
> Sǐ zhī tú shí yǒu sān,

Death | of 的 | disciple | 10 | has | 3,

Those who drift towards their places of death are three in ten.

> 人之生动之死地十有三。
> Rén zhī shēng dòng zhī sǐ dì shí yǒu sān.

People | of 的 | life | move | of 的 | death | place | 10 | has | 3.

▶ The total of these three types of people is 9 in 10, or 90%. The remaining 10%, those who care intensely for life, are the focus of the rest of the chapter.

Why? Because they live for life's sensations.

> 夫何故？以其生生之厚。
> Fū hé gù? Yǐ qí shēng shēng zhī hòu.

So | what | reason? | With | his/her | life | life | of 的 | thick/deep/rich.

▶ 厚 (hòu): *thick, large, profound, rich taste*, so literally, "they live for life's thickness"

It's said that one who cares intensely for life

> 盖闻善摄生者
> Gài wén shàn shè shēng zhě

About | hear | good | absorb | life | he/she

Can travel the land and not meet rhinos or tigers,

> 陆行不遇兕虎，
> Lù xíng bú yù sì hǔ,

Land | walk | not | meet | rhino | tiger,

Can enter battle without shield or sword.

> 入军不被甲兵。
> Rù jūn bú bèi jiǎbīng.

Enter | army | not | by | armor | weapons.

The rhino has no place to thrust its horn,
The tiger has no place to use its claws,

> 兕无所投其角，虎无所措其爪，
> Sì wú suǒ tóu qí jiǎo, hǔ wú suǒ cuò qí zhǎo,

Rhino | without | place | thrust | its | horn, |
Tiger | without | place | employ | its | claws,

The soldier's blade has no place to enter.

> 兵无所容其刃。
> Bīng wú suǒ róng qí rèn.

Soldier | without | place | appear | his | knife.

Why?
Because in him there is no place for death.

> 夫何故？以其无死地。
> Fū hé gù? Yǐ qí wú sǐ dì.

So | what | reason? |
Because | he | no | death | place.

51

Dao gives birth to them,
De raises them,
They begin to take shape,
Circumstances complete them.

So, of the ten thousand creatures,
None fail to respect Dao, and they honor De.

Respecting Dao,
Honoring De.

This is not commanded,
But is the natural way of things.

So, Dao gives life to them,
De raises them, grows them, nourishes them,
Shelters and heals them,
Supports and protects them,
Gives them birth but doesn't own them,
Acts but doesn't care about results,
Leads them but doesn't control them.

This is called Primal De.

Dao gives birth to them,
De raises them,
They begin to take shape,
Circumstances complete them.

> 道生之，德畜之，物形之，势成之。
> Dào shēng zhī, dé chù zhī, wù xíng zhī, shì chéng zhī.

Dao | birth/life | them, |
De | raise | them, |
Things/creatures | form | them, |
Power/force | completes | them.

▶ Each of these four lines end with 之 (zhī), which means *it* or *them* when appearing at the end of a phrase or sentence, and we see in the line below that this refers to the ten thousand things or creatures.

So, of the ten thousand creatures,
None fail to respect Dao, and they honor De.

> 是以万物，莫不尊道而贵德。
> Shìyǐ wànwù, mò bù zūn dào ér guì dé.

Therefore | ten thousand things/creatures, |
Not | without | respect | Dao | yet | respect/value | De.

Respecting Dao,
Honoring De,
This is not commanded,
But is the natural way of things.

> 道之尊，德之贵，夫莫之命，常自然。
> Dào zhī zūn, dé zhī guì, fū mò zhī mìng, cháng zìrán.

Dao | of 与 | respect, |
De | of 与 | respect/value, |

So | not | it | order/mandate |
Common/frequent | natural.

So, Dao gives life to them,
De raises them, grows them, nourishes them,

> 故，道生之，德畜之，长之，育之，
> Gù, dào shēng zhī, dé chù zhī, zhǎng zhī, yù zhī,

So, | Dao | birth | them, |
De | raise | them, | lead/grow | them, | educate/care for | them,

Shelters and heals them,
Supports and protects them,

> 亭之毒之，养之覆之，
> Tíng zhī dú zhī, yǎng zhī fù zhī,

Erect shelter | them | heals | them, |
Support | them | cover/protect | them,

▶ 毒 (dú): usually means *poisons*, but in this case the opposite, *heals*.

Gives them birth but doesn't own them,
Acts but doesn't care about results,

> 生而不有，为而不恃，
> Shēng ér bù yǒu, wéi ér bú shì,

Birth | but | not | have, | do | but | not | rely,

Leads them but doesn't control them.
This is called Primal De.

> 长而不宰。是谓玄德。
> Zhǎng ér bù zǎi. Shì wèi xuándé.

Lead/grow | but | not | govern. |
Is | called | Primal De.

▶ 玄德 (xuándé): *Primal De*, sometimes translated as *deep and mysterious De*

52

The world had a beginning,
This was the mother of the world.

When you find the mother,
You know her children.
Once you know her children,
You return to and stand with their mother.
 All your life, you're in no danger.

Block your senses, shut the gates,
All your life, you won't worry.

Open your senses, immerse yourself in your affairs,
All your life, you won't be rescued.

Seeing the small is called insight,
Maintaining the soft is called strength.

Use the light and come back to your insight.
Stay out of trouble and practice your normal routine.

The world had a beginning,
This was the mother of the world.

> 天下有始，以为天下母。
> Tiānxià yǒu shǐ, yǐwéi tiānxià mǔ.

Under heaven | has | beginning, | therefore | under heaven | mother.

▶ 母 (mǔ), *mother*, is often used to mean Dao.

When you find the mother,
You know her children.

> 既得其母，以知其子。
> Jì dé qí mǔ, yǐ zhī qí zi.

Already | get/find | his/her | mother, |
So | understand | his/her | child.

Once you know her children,
You return to and stand with their mother.

> 既知其子，复守其母。
> Jì zhī qí zi, fù shǒu qí mǔ.

Since | know | his/her | child, |
Return | protect | his/her | mother.

▶ 守 (shǒu): *protect, adhere to, stand with, hold one's ground*

All your life, you're in no danger.

> 没身，不殆。
> Mò shēn, bú dài.

Entire/whole | body/life, | no | danger.

Block your senses, shut the gates,

> 塞其兑，闭其门，
> Sè qí duì, bì qí mén,

> Block/stop up | her/her | cavity, | shut | his/her | gate,

All your life, you won't worry.

> 终身，不勤。
> Zhōngshēn, bù qín.

> Lifelong, | not | worry/work hard.

Open your senses, immerse yourself in your affairs,
All your life, you won't be rescued.

> 开其兑，济其事，终，身不救。
> Kāi qí duì, jì qí shì, zhōngshēn, bú jiù.

> Open | your | cavities, | stand in | your | things/affairs, |
> Lifelong, | not | saved.

Seeing the small is called insight,
Maintaining the soft is called strength.

> 见小曰明，守柔曰强。
> Jiàn xiǎo yuē míng, shǒu róu yuē qiáng.

> See | small | speaks | light, |
> Hold one's ground | soft | speaks | strong.

Use the light and come back to your insight.

> 用其光复归其明。
> Yòng qí guāng fùguī qí míng.

Use | his/her | light | return | his/her | bright/understand.

▶ This line and the next have identical structure, and many of the words rhyme.

Stay out of trouble and practice your normal routine.

> 无遗身殃是为习常。
> Wú yí shēn yāng shìwéi xí cháng.

Not have | lose | self/body | misfortune | therefore | practice | common.

53

If I have a little knowledge
While walking the great road,
I fear I might wander off.

The great road is very smooth,
But people like the side paths.

The royal court is well swept.
The fields are overgrown with weeds,
And the granaries are completely empty.

They wear colorful silks,
Carry sharp swords,
They stuff themselves with drink and food,
And have a surplus of riches.

This is called robbery and extravagance,
Not Dao!

If I have a little knowledge
While walking the great road,
I fear I might wander off.

> 使我介然有知行于大道，唯施是畏。
> Shǐ wǒ jiè rán yǒu zhī xíng yú dà dào, wéi shī shì wèi.

If | I | little | but | have | knowledge |
Travel | on | big | path, |
Only | veer off | is | fear/worry.

▶ 道 (Dào) has a literal meaning of *road* or *path*, of course, and that's the way it's used in these five lines, with "road" being a metaphor for the way of Dao.

The great road is very smooth,
But people like the side paths.

> 大道甚夷，而民好径。
> Dà dào shèn yí, ér mín hào jìng.

Great | path | considerably | smooth, |
But | citizens | like | narrow paths.

The royal court is well swept.
The fields are overgrown with weeds,
And the granaries are completely empty.

> 朝甚除。田甚芜，仓甚虚。
> Cháo shèn chú. Tián shèn wú, cāng shèn xū.

Royal court | very | well cleaned. |
Field | very | weedy, |
Granaries | very | empty.

▶ 除 (chú): in modern Chinese, *remove, divide, eliminate, wipe out,* so this might read "The royal court has been eliminated." But an older and more likely meaning is *well cleaned*, in the sense of *swept clean*.

They wear colorful silks,
Carry sharp swords,

> 服文彩，带利剑，
> Fú wén cǎi, dài lì jiàn,

Clothing | embroidered | colored silk, |
Carry on belt | sharp | sword,

They stuff themselves with drink and food,
And have a surplus of riches.

> 厌饮食，财货有余。
> Yàn yǐn shí, cái huò yǒu yú.

Satiate | drink | food, |
Wealth | goods | have | surplus.

This is called robbery and extravagance,
Not Dao!

> 是谓盗夸，非道也哉！
> Shì wèi dào kuā, fēi dào yě zāi!

This | called | steal/rob | extravagant, |
Not | Dao | <!> | <!>!

▶ 盗 (dào): *steal, rob, plunder*, but pronounced the same as 道 (Dào). So, a play on words: "This is dào but not Dào!"

54

Well established things are not easily uprooted.
Well held things are not easily pulled away.
That's why children and grandchildren continue to offer sacrifices.

Cultivate yourself, your De will be true.
Cultivate your family, its De will be enough.
Cultivate your village, its De will be long-lived.
Cultivate your nation, its De will be abundant.
Cultivate your world, its De will be everywhere.

So, use yourself to know yourself.
Use your family to know your family.
Use the village to know the village.
Use the nation to know the nation.
Use the world to know the world.

How do I know the world is like this?
Because of this.

Well established things are not easily uprooted,
Well held things are not easily pulled away.

> 善建不拔，善抱者不脱。
> Shàn jiàn bù bá, shàn bào zhě bù tuō.

Good | establish | not | pull out, |
Good | embrace | that which is | not | remove.

That's why children and grandchildren continue to offer sacrifices.

> 子孙以祭祀不辍。
> Zǐ sūn yǐ jìsì bú chuò.

Child | grandchild | thus | sacrifice | not | stop.

Cultivate yourself, your De will be true.

> 修之于身，其德乃真。
> Xiū zhī yú shēn, qí dé nǎi zhēn.

Cultivate | it | to | self/body, | your | De | thus | genuine.

▶ 修 (xiū): *cultivate, observe, study*, but also to repair or build

Cultivate your family, its De will be enough.

> 修之于家，其德乃余。
> Xiū zhī yú jiā, qí dé nǎi yú.

Cultivate | it | to | family, | its | De | thus | surplus.

Cultivate your village, its De will be long-lived.

> 修之于乡，其德乃长。
> Xiū zhī yú xiāng, qí dé nǎi cháng.

Cultivate | it | to | village, | its | De | thus | long.

Cultivate your nation, its De will be abundant.

> 修之于国，其德乃丰。
> Xiū zhī yú guó, qí dé nǎi fēng.

Cultivate | it | to | nation, | its | De | thus | abundant.

Cultivate your world, its De will be everywhere.

> 修之于天下，其德乃普。
> Xiū zhī yú tiānxià, qí dé nǎi pǔ.

Cultivate | it | to | under heaven, | its | De | thus | universal.

So, use yourself to know yourself,
Use your family to know your family,

> 故，以身观身，以家观家，
> Gù, yǐ shēn guān shēn, yǐ jiā guān jiā,

Thus, | use | self/body | to observe | self/body, | use | family | to observe | family,

Use the village to know the village,
Use the nation to know the nation,

> 以乡观乡，以国观国，
> Yǐ xiāng guān xiāng, yǐ guó guān guó,

Use | village | to observe | village, |
Use | nation | to observe | nation,

Use the world to know the world.

> 以天下观天下。
> Yǐ tiānxià guān tiānxià.

Use | under heaven | to observe | under heaven.

How do I know the world is like this?
Because of this.

> 吾何以知天下然哉？以此。
> Wú héyǐ zhī tiānxià rán zāi? Yǐ cǐ.

I | how | know | under heaven | then | <!>? | With | this.

55

One who holds the essence of De
Is like a newborn baby.

Wasps, scorpions and snakes don't sting him,
Savage beasts don't claw him,
Birds of prey do don't not seize him.

His bones are weak, his muscles are soft, but his grip is strong.
He has not yet known the union of female and male, yet he is erect.
His manhood is great!
He wails all day but doesn't get hoarse.
His harmony is great!

Knowing harmony is called unchanging,
Knowing the unchanging is called wisdom,
Trying to improve your life is called bad fortune.
Trying to control the Qi with your mind is called foolish strength.

Creatures grow strong, then age.
This is called not Dao.
Not Dao soon ends.

One who holds the essence of De
Is like a newborn baby.

> 含德之厚比于赤子。
> Hán dé zhī hòu bǐ yú chìzǐ.

Contain/hold in mouth | De | of⇆ | thick/deep/rich | Compared to | of | baby.

▶ 赤子 (chìzǐ): *a reddish child*, referring to the color of a newborn infant

Wasps, scorpions and snakes don't sting him,
Savage beasts don't claw him,
Birds of prey don't seize him.

> 蜂虿虺蛇不螫，猛兽不据，攫鸟不搏。
> Fēng chài huīshé bú shì, měng shòu bú jù, jué niǎo bù bó.

Bee/wasp | scorpion | viper | not | bite/puncture, |
Savage | beast | not | take, |
Snatch | bird | not | seize.

His bones are weak, his muscles are soft, but his grip is strong.

> 骨弱，筋柔，而握固。
> Gǔ ruò, jīn róu, ér wò gù.

Bones | fragile, | muscles | soft, | yet | grasp | strong.

He has not yet known the union of female and male, yet he is erect.
His manhood is great!

> 未知牝牡之合而全作，精之至也。
> Wèi zhī pìn mǔ zhī hé ér quán zuò, jīng zhī zhì yě.

Not yet | know | female | male | of⇆ | unite | not | maintain | arise/stand up/erect, |

Essence/spirit/semen | of ⇆ | extreme | <!>

▶ 精 (jīng): a positive word meaning *fine, refined, excellent, splendid, skilled,* and so on, but pertains to the male gender; can also mean *semen, essence of life*, or some aspect of male sexuality.

He wails all day but doesn't get hoarse.
His harmony is great!

> 终日号而不嗄。和之至也。
> Zhōngrì hào ér bù shà. Hé zhī zhì yě.

All day | howl/wail | but | not | hoarse, |
Harmony | of ⇆ | extremely | <!>

▶ 和 (hé) means *and* in modern Chinese, but here, it has an older meaning of *blend, mix together, harmonious, chime in, "join in the singing."*

Knowing harmony is called unchanging,
Knowing the unchanging is called wisdom,

> 知和曰常，知常曰明，
> Zhī hé yuē cháng, zhī cháng yuē míng,

Know | harmony | called | common/frequent, |
Know | common/frequent | called | bright,

Trying to improve your life is called bad fortune,
Trying to control the Qi with your mind is called foolish strength.

> 益生曰祥，心使气曰强。
> Yì shēng yuē xiáng, xīn shǐ qì yuē qiáng.

Benefit | life/birth | called | lucky omen, |
Heart/mind | enabled | qi | called | powerful.

▶ 强 (qiáng) means *strong* and *powerful,* but also *forceful* and *rigid.* Trying to control *qi* certainly require strength, but it is also foolish.

Creatures grow strong, then age.
This is called not Dao.
Not Dao soon ends.

> 物壮则老。谓之不道。不道早已。
> Wù zhuàng zé lǎo. Wèi zhī bú dào. Bú dào zǎo yǐ.

Creatures | strong | then | old. |
Called | it | not | Dao. |
Not | Dao | early | stop.

56

One who knows doesn't speak,
One who speaks doesn't know.

Block your senses, shut the gates,
Blunt your sharpness,
Unravel your tangles,
Soften your brightness,
Be the same as dust.
This is called a deep sameness.

So, you can't have it and be intimate,
You can't have it and stand apart.

You can't have it and benefit,
You can't have it and cause harm,

You can't have it and be noble,
You can't have it and be worthless.

So, in the world you will lead.

One who knows doesn't speak,
One who speaks doesn't know.

> 知者不言，言者不知。
> Zhī zhě bù yán, yán zhě bù zhī.

Have knowledge | he/she | not | speak, |
Speak | he/she | not | know.

Block your senses, shut the gates,

> 塞其兑，闭其门，
> Sè qí duì, bì qí mén,

Block/seal | it | cavity, | shut/close | it | gate,

Blunt your sharpness,

Unravel your tangles,

Soften your brightness,

> 挫其锐，解其分，和其光，
> Cuò qí ruì, jiě qí fèn, hé qí guāng,

Grind/push down | it | sharp, |
Simplify/solve | it | complications/difference, |
Harmony | it | bright,

▶ The second line, 解其分 (jiě qí fèn), is difficult to render exactly in English, because of the subtle meanings of 解 and 分, and because the pronoun in between, 其 (qí), can mean *its*, *his*, *her*, or *your*. This line has been variously translated as "untie all tangles," "unravel its complications," "simplify your problems," "untangle your knots," "untie the tangles," and even "resolve your differences."

Be the same as dust.
This is called a deep sameness.

> 同其尘。是谓玄同。
> Tóng qí chén. Shì wèi xuán tóng.

Same | it | dust. |
Is | called | deep | same.

So, you can't have it and be intimate,
You can't have it and stand apart.

> 故，不可得而亲，不可得而疏。
> Gù, bùkě dé ér qīn, bùkě dé ér shū.

So, | cannot | have/get | and | intimate, |
Cannot | have/get | and | neglect.

▶ In these lines, "it" might be Dao, or De.

You can't have it and benefit,
You can't have it and cause harm.

> 不可得而利，不可得而害。
> Bùkě dé ér lì, bùkě dé ér hài.

Cannot | have/get | like | lucky/useful, |
Cannot | have/get | like | harm.

You can't have it and be noble,
You can't have it and be worthless.

> 不可得而贵，不可得而贱。
> Bùkě dé ér guì, bùkě dé ér jiàn.

Cannot | have/get | like | high/valuable, |
Cannot | have/get | like | low/worthless.

So, in the world you will lead.

> 故，为天下贵。
> Gù, wéi tiānxià guì.

So, | as | under heaven | high/exalted/high rank.

▶ Here, 为 (wéi) means *as*, not *act* as it is used elsewhere.

▶ This has the sense of "people will see you as a noble leader."

57

Use justice when governing a nation,
Use surprise tactics when commanding troops,
Use no striving to capture the world.

How do I know this?
Because of this:

The more fears and taboos there are in the world,
The poorer the citizens become.

The more sharp weapons the citizens have,
The more nations and families fall into darkness.

The more talented and clever the people are,
The more unexplained things happen.

The more new laws are proclaimed,
The more bandits there are.

So, the sage says:
I do not act, and the citizens obey.
I enjoy peace, and the citizens become just.
I do nothing, and the citizens become wealthy.
I have no desire, and the citizens become simple and honest.

Use justice when governing a nation,
Use surprise tactics when commanding troops,
Use no striving to capture the world.

> 以正治国，以奇用兵，以无事取天下。
> Yǐ zhèng zhì guó, yǐ qí yòng bīng, yǐ wúshì qǔ tiānxià.

Use | straight/just | rule | nation, |
Use | strange/uncanny | use | troops, |
Use | nothing | catch | under heaven.

▸ 奇 (qí): *strange, uncanny, occult*. Used twice in this chapter. Here, it means surprising or unexpected tactics used in battle. Later on, it means mysterious things that occur despite the cleverness of the citizens.

How do I know this? Because of this:

> 吾何以知其然哉？以此：
> Wú héyǐ zhī qí rán zāi? Yǐ cǐ:

I | how | know | it | like that | <!>? | Because | this:

The more fears and taboos there are in the world,
The poorer the citizens become.

> 天下多忌讳，而民弥贫。
> Tiānxià duō jì huì, ér mín mí pín.

Under heaven | much | fear/jealous | taboo, |
And | citizens | extensive | poor.

The more sharp weapons the citizens have,
The more nations and families fall into darkness.

> 民多利器，国家滋昏。
> Mín duō lì qì, guójiā zī hūn.

Citizens | much | sharp | instruments, |
Nation | grow | nightfall.

The more talented and clever the people are,
The more unexplained things happen.

> 人多伎巧，奇物滋起。
> Rén duō jì qiǎo, qí wù zī qǐ.

People | much | talent | clever, |
Strange/uncanny | thing/creature | grow | stand up.

The more new laws are proclaimed,
The more bandits there are.

> 法令滋彰，盗贼多有。
> Fǎ lìng zī zhāng, dào zéi duō yǒu.

Law | decree | grow | clear, |
Bandit | thief | more | have.

So, the sage says:
I do not act, and the citizens obey.

> 故圣人云：我无为，而民自化。
> Gù shèngrén yún: Wǒ wúwéi, ér mín zì huà.

So | sage | says: |
I | empty action, | then | citizens | self | follow/obey.

I enjoy peace, and the citizens become just.

> 我好静，而民自正。
> Wǒ hào jìng, ér mín zì zhèng.

I | like | quiet/gentle, | then | citizens | self | straight.

I do nothing, and the citizens become wealthy.

> 我无事，而民自富。
> Wǒ wú shì, ér mín zì fù.

I | without | things/matters, | then | citizens | self | abundant/wealthy.

I have no desire, and the citizens become simple and honest.

> 我无欲，而民自朴。
> Wǒ wú yù, ér mín zì pǔ.

I | without | desire, | then | citizens | self | simple/honest.

▶ The last line could be "I have no desire, and the citizens return to their natural state of being the uncarved block."

58

If government doesn't interfere,
Its citizens will be honest.

If government is suspicious,
Its citizens will be dissatisfied.

Disaster! It is rooted in good fortune.
Good fortune! It lies hidden in disaster.
Who knows its reach?
Nobody knows.

Justice becomes evil,
Goodness also becomes evil.
The people have been bewitched for a long time.

Thus, the sage is
Honest but not critical,
Strong but not hurtful,
Straightforward but not pushy,
Brilliant but not flashy.

If government doesn't interfere,
Its citizens will be honest.

> 其政闷闷，其民淳淳。
> Qí zhèng mènmèn, qí mín chúnchún.

Their | government | loose/relaxed, |
The | citizens | honest.

If government is suspicious,
Its citizens will be dissatisfied.

> 其政察察，其民缺缺。
> Qí zhèng cháchá, qí mín quēquē.

Their | government | inspect/scrutinize, |
The | citizens | dissatisfied.

▶ These four lines all have adjectives that are doubled: 闷闷, 淳淳, 察察 and 缺缺. Doubling makes the adjective stronger, like adding "very."

Disaster! It is rooted in good fortune.
Good fortune! It lies hidden in disaster.

> 祸兮福之所倚。福兮祸之所伏。
> Huò xī fú zhī suǒyǐ. Fú xī huò zhī suǒfú.

Disaster | <!> | good fortune | of⇆ | reliance. |
Good fortune | <!> | disaster | of⇆ | conceal/hide.

▶ Note the beautiful symmetry in the sounds of these two lines, including the use of two different words pronounced identically: 福 (fú), *good fortune*, and 伏 (fú), *conceal* or *hide*.

Who knows its reach?
Nobody knows.

> 孰知其极？其无正。
> Shú zhī qí jí? Qí wú zhèng.

Who | knows | its | extreme? | They | not have | standard/norm.

▶ The last line could be read "Who knows the extent of this idea?"

Justice becomes evil,
Goodness also becomes evil.

> 正复为奇，善复为妖。
> Zhèng fù wéi qí, shàn fù wéi yāo.

Straight/correct| become | as | evil/strange, |
Goodness | become | do | evil/weird.

▶ 奇 (qí) and 妖 (yāo) can both be translated as *evil*.

The people have been bewitched for a long time.

> 人之迷其日固久。
> Rén zhī mí qí rì gù jiǔ.

People | of 与 | bewitch/charm | their | day | already | long time.

Thus, the sage is:
Honest but not critical,
Strong but not hurtful,

> 是以，圣人：方而不割，廉而不刿，
> Shìyǐ, shèngrén: fāng ér bù gē, lián ér bú guì,

Therefore, | sage: |
Upright | yet | not | cut off/mow down, |
Honorable | yet | not | cut,

Straightforward but not pushy,
Brilliant but not flashy.

> 直而不肆，光而不耀。
> Zhí ér bú sì, guāng ér bú yào.

Straight | yet | not | presumptuous/wanton, |
Bright light | yet | not | shine.

59

Whether governing people or serving heaven,
Be like a farmer who stores rice.

Storing your rice is called preparing early.
Preparing early is called accumulating De.
Accumulate De, and everything can be overcome.

When everything can be overcome, there are no limits.
When there are no limits, you can have the nation.
When you have the mother of the nation, you can last a long time.

This is called having deep roots and firm ground,
The Dao of long life and lasting vision.

Whether governing people or serving heaven,
Be like a farmer who stores rice.

> 治人事天，莫若啬。
> Zhì rén shì tiān, mòruò sè.

Rule | people | serve | heaven, |
Better | farmer/store rice.

▶ 啬 (sè): in modern Chinese, *thrifty* or *stingy*, but the older meaning is to store rice, or someone who stores rice, *a farmer*.

Storing your rice is called preparing early.

> 夫唯啬是谓早服。
> Fū wéi sè shì wèi zǎo fú.

So | only | farmer/store rice | is | called | early | prepare.

▶ "Store rice" is a metaphor for how an elightened ruler governs a country, manages the economy, collects taxes, administers justice, wages war, etc.

Preparing early is called accumulating De.

> 早服谓之重积德。
> Zǎo fú wèi zhī chóng jī dé.

Early | prepare | called | it | repeat | accumulate | De.

Accumulate De, and everything can be overcome.

> 重积德，则无不克。
> Chóng jī dé, zé wú bú kè.

Repeat | accumulate | De, | therefore | not have | not | overcome.

When everything can be overcome, there are no limits.

> 无不克，则莫知其极。
> Wú bú kè, zé mò zhī qí jí.

Not have | not | overcome, | therefore | do not | know | its | extreme limit.

When there are no limits, you can have the nation.

> 莫知其极，可以有国。
> Mò zhī qí jí, kěyǐ yǒu guó.

Do not | know | its | extreme limit, | can | have | nation.

When you have the mother of the nation, you can last a long time.

> 有国之母，可以长久。
> Yǒu guózhī mǔ, kěyǐ chángjiǔ.

Have | nation's | mother, | can | for a long time.

▶ In China, the earth is the mother of the nation.

This is called having deep roots and firm ground,
The Dao of long life and lasting vision.

> 是谓深根固柢，长生久视之道。
> Shì wèi shēn gēn gù dǐ, chángshēng jiǔ shì zhī dào.

Is | called | deep | root | solidified | base/ground, | Long life | long | look at | of 与 | Dao.

60

Governing a great nation is like cooking a small fish.

Because Dao has come into the world,
Death and decay have no spiritual power.

Not that death and decay have no spiritual power,
But its spiritual power doesn't hurt people.

Not only does its spiritual power not hurt people,
The sage also doesn't hurt people.

These two don't hurt each other,
Therefore De returns!

Governing a great nation is like cooking a small fish.

> 治大国若烹小鲜。
> Zhì dàguó ruò pēng xiǎo xiān.

Administer | great nation | like | cook by frying | small | seafood.

Because Dao has come into the world,
Death and decay have no spiritual power.

> 以道莅天下，其鬼不神。
> Yǐ dào lì tiānxià, qí guǐ bù shén.

With | Dao | arrive | under heaven, |
Its | ghost/devil | not | spirit/god.

▶ This chapter talks about two supernatural concepts: 鬼 (guǐ) is earthly, it has to do with death, and can be translated as *evil, ghost, demon, devil, souls of the deceased, returning to the earth upon death*. Its counterpart, 神 (shén), is heavenly, it has to do with life and can be a force (*spiritual power*) or a being infused with that force (*a godlike spirit, a deity, a magical or divine spirit*). So "Death and decay have no spiritual power" could be expressed in more detail as "The souls of the deceased, when they arise from the ground, have no divine spirit or power."

Not that death and decay have no spiritual power,
But its spiritual power doesn't hurt people.

> 非其鬼不神，其神不伤人。
> Fēi qí guǐ bù shén, qí shén bù shāng rén.

Not | its | ghost/devil | not | spirit/god, |
Its | spirit/god | not | injure | people.

Not only does its spiritual power not hurt people,
The sage also doesn't hurt people.

> 非其神不伤人，圣人亦不伤人。
> Fēi qí shén bù shāng rén, shèngrén yì bù shāng rén.

Not | its | spirit | not | injure | people, |
Sage | also | not | injure | people.

These two don't hurt each other,
Therefore De returns!

> 夫两不相伤，故德交归焉。
> Fū liǎng bù xiāng shāng, gù dé jiāoguī yān.

So | both | not | each other | injure, |
Therefore | De | returns | <!>.

▶ "These two" are the spirit and the sage.

▶ In the last line, 交归 (jiāoguī) means *to return, to give back to, to be cared for by, to gather together*. Return to what, give back to whom? Perhaps, De returns goodness to the people.

61

A great nation is the valley to which all waters flow,
The confluence of the world,
The female of the world.

The female uses stillness to conquer the male,
She uses stillness to remain low.

So, a great nation becomes lower than a small nation,
And thus wins over the small nation.
A small nation becomes lower than a great nation,
And thus is won over by the great nation.

So, some become low to win over,
Some become low to be won over.

A great nation doesn't want to be too controlling,
A small nation doesn't want to be too submissive.

So, for both nations to get what they want,
The great nation should remain low.

A great nation is the valley to which all waters flow,
The confluence of the world,
The female of the world.

> 大国者下流，天下之交，天下之牝。
> Dàguó zhě xià liú, tiānxià zhī jiāo, tiānxià zhī pìn.

Great nation | it | low | flow (stream), |
Under heaven | of 与 | intersect/merge, |
Under heaven | of 与 | female.

The female uses stillness to conquer the male,
She uses stillness to remain low.

> 牝常以静胜牡，以静为下。
> Pìn cháng yǐ jìng shèng mǔ, yǐ jìng wéi xià.

Female | common/frequent | use | quiet/still | better than | male, |
Use | quiet/still | be/remain | low.

▶ In this chapter, the common word 下 (xià) is translated as *low*, but it's really *relatively low*, that is, *low in comparison with the other*.

▶ These two lines remind us of how the feminine (yīn) can, by yielding, conquer the male (yáng). In the rest of the chapter, this is applied to the relationship between small (yīn) and large (yáng) nations.

So, a great nation becomes lower than a small nation,
And thus wins over the small nation.

> 故大国以下小国，则取小国。
> Gù dàguó yǐ xià xiǎoguó, zé qǔ xiǎoguó.

So | great nation | use | low | small nation, |
Then | cut off | small nation.

▶ 取 (qǔ): *to unify through conquest.* Other translations include *catch, take, gain possession of, defeat in battle, take a wife, achieve an easy victory.*

A small nation becomes lower than a great nation,
And thus is won over by the great nation.

> 小国以下大国，则取大国。
> Xiǎoguó yǐ xià dàguó, zé qǔ dàguó.

Small nation | use | low | great nation, |
Then | cut off | great nation.

▶ Interestingly, the previous two lines have identical structure and both use 大 (qǔ), but they have opposite meanings! In the first line, 大 means "to take over," but in the second, it means "to please through submission." This is confirmed by the next two lines, which summarize the previous two.

So, some become low to win over,
Some become low to be won over.

> 故或下以取，或下而取。
> Gù huò xià yǐ qǔ, huò xià ér qǔ.

So | sometimes | low | gets | cut off, |
Sometimes | low | then | cut off.

A great nation doesn't want to be too controlling,
A small nation doesn't want to be too submissive.

> 大国不过欲兼畜人，小国不过欲入事人。
> Dàguó bùguò yù jiān chù rén, xiǎoguó bùguò yù rù shì rén.

Great nation | only | desires | bring in | herd/gathering | people, |
Small nation | only | desires | get into | serving | people.

So, for both nations to get what they want,
The great nation should remain low.

> 夫两者各得其所欲，大者宜为下。
> Fū liǎng zhě gè dé qí suǒyù, dà zhě yí wéi xià.

So | both | that which is | each | obtain | their | desire, |
Great | that which is | suitable | be/remain | low.

62

Dao is the deep mystery of the ten thousand things,
Treasure for a person with virtue,
Protection for a person without virtue.

Use pretty words to become popular,
Use good deeds to win respect,
But how can those without virtue give up on it?

So, when installing the emperor on his throne,
Or appointing the three nobles,
You can offer jade disks and horse-drawn carriages,
But it's not as good as sitting and entering the Dao.

Why did the ancients value the Dao so highly?
Didn't they say,
Seek and you will find it,
And your crimes will be erased?

Thus, Dao becomes valuable to the world.

Dao is the deep mystery of the ten thousand things,

> 道者万物之奥，
> Dào zhě wànwù zhī ào,

Dao | that which is | ten thousand things/creatures | of 之 | mystery/profound,

Treasure for a person with virtue,
Protection for a person without virtue.

> 善人之宝，不善人之所保。
> Shàn rén zhī bǎo, bù shàn rén zhī suǒ bǎo.

Good/virtue | person | of 之 | treasure, |
Not | good/virtue | person | of 之 | \<make noun\> | protection.

▶ 宝 (bǎo): *treasure*. Historically, the southwest corner of the house where worship occurred and grain was stored.

▶ These two lines rhyme, ending with different words that have exactly the same pronounciation: 宝 (bǎo), *treasure*, and 保 (bǎo), *protection*.

Use pretty words to become popular,
Use good deeds to win respect,

> 美言可以市，尊行可以加人，
> Měi yán kěyǐ shì, zūn xíng kěyǐ jiā rén,

Beautiful | words | can | (to) market, |
Respect | behavior | can | increase | people,

▶ The first line, "beautiful words can market," means "use beautiful words in a marketplace to get people to like you and buy your goods."

But how can those without virtue give up on it?

> 人之不善何弃之有？
> Rén zhī bú shàn hé qì zhī yǒu?

People | of 之 | not | good | how | reject/abandon | it | have?

▸ "it" is Dao.

▸ The first three lines tell us about Dao. The next three lines tell us the same things about De, the way of virtue for one who understands Dao.

So, when installing the emperor on his throne,
Or appointing the three nobles,

> 故立天子，置三公，
> Gù lì tiān zǐ, zhì sān gōng,

So | enthrone ruler | son of heaven, |
Establish | three | nobles,

▸ The three nobles are 太师 (tàishī) a teacher of the emperor's young heir, 太傅 (tàifù) an emperor's advisor, and 太保 (tàibǎo) a young emperor's guardian.

You can offer jade disks and horse-drawn carriages,
But it's not as good as sitting and entering the Dao.

> 虽有拱璧以先驷马，不如坐进此道。
> Suī yǒu gǒng bì yǐ xiān sìmǎ, bùrú zuò jìn cǐ dào.

Even though | have | hold in both hands | jade | as | first/before | carriage pulled by a team of four horses, |
Not like | sit | enter | this | Dao.

▸ 拱(gǒng): *to hold something with hands clasped together*. In this context, "to humbly offer something."

▸ 坐 (zuò): *to sit*, but here it means to sit or kneel (or kowtow, a traditional bow) in a humble position, mirroring the humble offering of gifts in the previous line.

▶ 璧 (bì): *a decorative jade annulus*, a disk with a hole in the center, used since ancient times. It symbolizes a covering sky revolving around a central axis. During Laozi's time, bì disks were given by the leader of a defeated army to the victors as a sign of their submission.

Why did the ancients value the Dao so highly?

> 古之所以贵此道者何?
> Gǔ zhīsuǒyǐ guì cǐ dào zhě hé?

Ancient | the reason for | valuable | this | Dao | that which is | <!>?

Didn't they say,
Seek and you will find it,
And your crimes will be erased?

> 不曰：以求得，有罪以免耶?
> Bù yuē: Yǐ qiú dé, yǒu zuì yǐ miǎn yé?

Not | say: |
From | seek | get, |
Have | crime/sin/vice/evil | can | exempt/avoid | <!>?

Thus, Dao becomes valuable to the world.

> 故为天下贵。
> Gù wéi tiānxià guì.

So | as | under heaven | valuable.

63

Act without acting,
Work without getting involved,
Taste without tasting.

No matter how great or how often,
Repay injury with De.

Overcome the hard while it is still easy,
Achieve the large while it is still tiny.

The world's difficult things surely begin easy.
The world's great things surely begin tiny.

Therefore, the sage in the end sees nothing as great,
And so can accomplish great things.

Make promises lightly and few will trust you.
Expect things to be easy and they will be difficult.

Therefore, the sage sees everything as difficult,
So in the end nothing is difficult!

Act without acting,
Work without getting involved,
Taste without tasting.

> 为无为，事无事，味无味。
> Wéiwúwéi, shì wú shì, wèi wú wèi.

Act without acting, |
Work/serve | without | things/matters, |
Taste | without | taste.

▶ These three lines work beautifully in Chinese, where the same word 事 (shì) can be a verb ("act") and also a noun ("action"). Not quite as easy in English!

▶ There's a nice play on words here: the first and third lines are pronounced nearly the same, only differing in tone: wéi wúwéi and wèi wúwèi.

No matter how great or how often,
Repay injury with De.

> 大小多少，报怨以德。
> Dà xiǎo duō shǎo, bào yuàn yǐ dé.

Large | small | much | few, |
Repay | hatred/resentment | with | De.

▶ In Chinese, combining two opposites gives the measurement of that thing. For example, large + small = size; much + few = quantity. So the first line is, literally, "Size quantity."

Overcome the hard while it is still easy,
Achieve the large while it is still tiny.

> 图难于其易，为大于其细。
> Tú nán yú qí yì, wéi dà yú qí xì.

Pursue/overcome | difficult | from | its | easy, |
Make | large | from | its | tiny.

The world's difficult things surely begin easy.
The world's great things surely begin tiny.

> 天下难事必作于易。天下大事必作于细。
> Tiānxià nán shì bì zuò yú yì. Tiānxià dà shì bì zuò yú xì.

Under heaven | difficult | matter/thing | surely | do | while | easy. |
Under heaven | large | matter/thing | surely | do | while | tiny.

Therefore, the sage in the end sees nothing as great,
And so can accomplish great things.

> 是以圣人终不为大，故能成其大。
> Shìyǐ shèngrén zhōng bù wéi dà, gù néng chéng qí dà.

Therefore | sage | in the end | not | make | large/great, |
So | can | finish | his | large/great.

Make promises lightly and few will trust you.
Expect things to be easy and they will be difficult.

> 夫轻诺必寡信。多易必多难。
> Fū qīng nuò bì guǎ xìn. Duō yì bì duō nán.

So | light | promise | certainly | few | trust. |
Much | easy | surely | much | difficult.

Therefore, the sage sees everything as difficult,
So in the end nothing is difficult!

> 是以圣人犹难之，故终无难矣。
> Shìyǐ shèngrén yóu nán zhī, gù zhōng wú nán yǐ.

Therefore | sage | very | difficult | it, |
Therefore | in the end | not have | difficulty | <!>.

64

Things at rest are easy to hold,
Things not yet been revealed are easy to plan for,
Brittle things are easily shattered,
Small things are easily scattered.

Deal with things before they appear,
Set things in order before they are in chaos.

A tree too big to embrace is born from a tiny shoot.
A tower of nine stories rises from a heap of dirt.
A journey of a thousand miles begins with a single step.

Act and you'll be defeated,
Grasp and you'll lose.

Thus the sage
Doesn't act, so he is not defeated,
Doesn't grasp, so he doesn't lose.

People often fail when they've almost completed their tasks.
So, be as careful at the end as in the beginning,
Then you will not ruin your affairs.

Thus the sage:
Pursues what others don't pursue,
Has no interest in rare goods,
Learns what others don't learn,
Corrects the mistakes of others,
Helps the ten thousand creatures to what is natural,
But doesn't dare to act.

Things at rest are easy to hold,
Things not yet been revealed are easy to plan for,

> 其安易持，其未兆易谋，
> Qí ān yì chí, qí wèi zhào yì móu,

Its | stable/steady | easy | maintain, |
Its | not | sign/omen | easy | plan,

Brittle things are easily shattered,
Small things are easily scattered.

> 其脆易泮，其微易散。
> Qí cuì yì pàn, qí wēi yì sàn.

Its | fragile | easy | fall apart, |
Its | small | easy | disperse.

Deal with things before they appear,
Set things in order before they are in chaos.

> 为之于未有，治之于未乱。
> Wéi zhī yú wèi yǒu, zhì zhī yú wèi luàn.

Act | of 与 | to | not yet | have, |
Rule | of 与 | to | not yet | chaos.

A tree too big to embrace is born from a tiny shoot.
A tower of nine stories rises from a heap of dirt.

> 合抱之木生于毫末。九层之台起于累土。
> Hé bào zhī mù shēng yú háo mò. Jiǔ céng zhī tái qǐ yú lěi tǔ.

Gather | embrace | of 与 | tree | birth | from | fine hair | insignificant. |
Nine | story | of 与 | tower | rise up | from | heap/stack | soil.

▶ 台 (tái): not really a tower, but *a man-made hill* common in ancient China that can be climbed to view the surrounding countryside

A journey of a thousand miles begins with a single step.

> 千里之行始于足下。
> Qiān lǐ zhī xíng shǐ yú zúxià.

Thousand | li | of⇆ | go | begin | from | underfoot.

▶ One of the most famous lines in the DDJ. Literally, it reads "A journey of a thousand *li* begins with the road that's under your foot." In other words, a great journey starts right where you are.

▶ One 里 (lǐ), *a Chinese mile*, was in Laozi's time about a quarter of a mile. The 里 character is a combination of 田 (tián), *field*, and 土 (tǔ), *earth*, meaning the length of a village.

Act and you'll be defeated,
Grasp and you'll lose.

> 为者败之，执者失之。
> Wéi zhě bài zhī, zhí zhě shī zhī.

Act | that which is | be defeated | it, | hold | that which is | lose | it.

Thus the sage:
Doesn't act, so he is not defeated,
Doesn't grasp, so he doesn't lose.

> 是以圣人：无为，故无败，无执，故无失。
> Shìyǐ shèngrén: wúwéi, gù wú bài, wú zhí, gù wú shī.

Therefore | sage: |
Empty action, | thus | not have | be defeated, |
Not have | hold, | thus | not have | lose.

People often fail when they've almost completed their tasks.

> 民之从事常于几成而败之。
> Mín zhī cóngshì cháng yú jī chéng ér bài zhī.

Citizens | of⇆ | engaged | frequent | of | almost | completed | yet | be defeated | it.

So, be as careful at the end as in the beginning,
Then you will not ruin your affairs.

> 慎终如始，则无败事。
> Shèn zhōng rú shǐ, zé wú bài shì.

Be careful | in the end | as/like | beginning, |
Then | not have | be defeated | thing/matter.

Thus the sage:
Pursues what others don't pursue,

> 是以圣人：欲不欲，
> Shìyǐ shèngrén: yù bú yù,

Therefore | sage: |
Desire | not | desire,

Has no interest in rare goods,
Learns what others don't learn,

> 不贵难得之货，学不学，
> Bú guì nán dé zhī huò, xué bù xué,

Not | valuable | difficult | gain | of⇆ | goods, |
Learn | not | learn,

Corrects the mistakes of others,

> 复众人之所过，
> Fù zhòngrén zhī suǒ guò,

Rescue/recover | crowd | of ⇆ | about | mistake,

Helps the ten thousand creatures to what is natural,
But doesn't dare to act.

> 以辅万物之自然，而不敢为。
> Yǐ fǔ wànwù zhī zìrán, ér bù gǎn wéi.

So as to | help | ten thousand things/creatures | of ⇆ | nature, | But | not | dare | act.

▶ That is, doesn't dare to act for selfish motives.

65

The ancients acted in Dao,
Not to give the citizens knowledge,
But to let them become simple.

Citizens are hard to govern
When they have too much knowledge.

So, using knowledge to govern the nation is thievery.
Not using knowledge to govern the nation is good fortune.

Understand these two and use them as principles.
 Always understand these principles,
This is called Primal De.
Primal De is deep and everlasting!

When creatures return,
They reach their greatest harmony.

The ancients acted in Dao,
Not to give the citizens knowledge,
But to let them become simple.

> 古之善为道者，非以明民，将以愚之。
> Gǔ zhī shàn wéi dào zhě, fēi yǐ míng mín, jiāng yǐ yú zhī.

Ancient | of⇆ | good | act | Dao | that which is, |
Oppose | by | wisdom | people, |
Do | by | stupid | it.

▶ It's hard to put a positive spin on 愚 (yú); the word means *stupid, foolish.* But here Laozi flips the meaning and uses it as *simple,* as in, "the ancients kept the citizens in a state of blissful simplicity."

Citizens are hard to govern
When they have too much knowledge.

> 民之难治以其智多。
> Mín zhī nán zhì yǐ qí zhì duō.

Citizens | of⇆ | difficult | govern | because | their | wisdom | more.

▶ In this line and the next three, 智 (zhì) mean *knowledge* in the sense of *cunning, tricky, clever,* not the true wisdom that comes from Dao.

So, using knowledge to govern the nation is thievery.

> 故以智治国国之贼。
> Gù yǐ zhì zhì guó guó zhī zéi.

So | use | wisdom | govern | nation | nation | of⇆ | thievery/banditry.

Not using knowledge to govern the nation is good fortune.

> 不以智治国，国之福。
> Bù yǐ zhì zhì guó, guó zhī fú.

Not | use | wisdom | govern | nation, | nation | of ⇆ | good fortune.

Understand these two and use them as principles.

> 知此两者亦稽式。
> Zhī cǐ liǎng zhě yì jīshì.

Know | these | two | that which is | also | examples/methods/principles.

Always understand these principles,
This is called Primal De.

> 常知稽式，是谓玄德。
> Cháng zhī jīshì, shì wèi xuándé.

Frequent/common | know | examples/methods/principles, | Is | said | Primal De.

Primal De is deep and everlasting!

> 玄德深矣，远矣！
> Xuándé shēn yǐ, yuǎn yǐ!

Primal De | deep/far | <!>, | long/far away | <!>!

▶ 远 (yuǎn): *lasting a long time,* also *being far away*

When creatures return,
They reach their greatest harmony.

> 与物反矣，然后乃至大顺。
> Yǔ wù fǎn yǐ, ránhòu nǎi zhì dà shùn.

With | thing/creature | return | <!>, |
Afterwards | can | reach | great | obey.

▶ That is, "when creatures return to the state of simplicity, without knowledge …"

66

Rivers and seas can be kings of the hundred valleys,
Because they are good at lying low,
And so, they can be kings of the hundred valleys.

So, if the sage wants to be above the citizens,
He must speak as if he is lower than them.

If the sage wants to be in front of the citizens,
He must follow behind them.

Thus the sage
Lives above them, but the citizens aren't burdened.
Lives in front of them, but the citizens aren't harmed.

The world will support him, and won't tire of him.

He doesn't strive,
So no one in the world can strive against him.

Rivers and seas can be kings of the hundred valleys,

> 江海所以能为百谷王者，
> Jiāng hǎi suǒyǐ néng wéi bǎi gǔ wángzhě,

    River | ocean | so | can | be regarded as | one hundred | valley | kings,

Because they are good at lying low,
And so, they can be kings of the hundred valleys.

> 以其善下之，故能为百谷王。
> Yǐ qí shàn xià zhī, gù néng wéi bǎi gǔ wáng.

    With | he/she/it | good | low | it, |
    Thus | can | serve as | hundred | valley | kings.

So, if the sage wants to be above the citizens,
He must speak as if he is lower than them.

> 是以圣人欲上民，必以言下之。
> Shìyǐ shèngrén yù shàng mín, bì yǐ yán xià zhī.

    Therefore | the sage | desires | top/above | citizens, |
    Surely | by | speak | under | them.

If the sage wants to be in front of the citizens,
He must follow behind them.

> 欲先民，必以身后之。
> Yù xiān mín, bì yǐ shēn hòu zhī.

    Desire | first/in front of | citizens, |
    Surely | by | body/self | behind | them.

Thus the sage
Lives above them, but the citizens aren't burdened.

> 是以圣人处上，而民不重。
> Shìyǐ shèngrén chǔ shàng, ér mín bù chóng.

Therefore | the sage |
Resides | top, | yet | citizens | not | heavy.

Lives in front of them, but the citizens aren't harmed.

> 处前，而民不害。
> Chǔ qián, ér mín bú hài.

Resides | in front of, | but | citizens | not | injure.

The world will support him, and won't tire of him.

> 是以天下乐推，而不厌。
> Shìyǐ tiānxià lè tuī, ér bú yàn.

Therefore | under heaven | happy | push forward, | but | not | reject/detest.

He doesn't strive,

So no one in the world can strive against him.

> 以其不争，故天下莫能与之争。
> Yǐ qí bù zhēng, gù tiānxià mò néng yǔ zhī zhēng.

With | he/she | not | strive, |
So | under heaven | no one | can | with | he/she | strive.

67

Everyone in the world says my Dao is great,
But it's like nothing else.

The reason it's great is because it's like nothing else.
If it was like everything else all this time,
It would be insignificant!

Now I have three treasures that I hold and protect:
The first is compassion,
The second is frugality,
The third is not daring to be in front.

Because I'm kind I can be brave.
Because I'm frugal I can be generous.
Because I'm not in front, I can lead others.

Today, people abandon kindness, trying to be brave.
Abandon frugality, trying to be generous.
Abandon following, trying to be in front.
This is death!

Kindness in battle brings victory,
In defense it brings strength.
Heaven will rescue you,
And with kindness protect you.

Everyone in the world says my Dao is great,
But it's like nothing else.

> 天下皆谓我道大，似不肖。
> Tiānxià jiē wèi wǒ dào dà, sì bú xiào.

Under heaven | all | say | I/my | Dao | great, |
Similar | not | look like.

▶ 我 (wǒ) means *I* or *me*, but also shorthand for *my* or *mine*, which is how it's used here.

The reason it's great is because it's like nothing else.

> 夫唯大故似不肖。
> Fū wéi dà gù sì bú xiào.

So | only | great | therefore | similar | not | look like.

If it was like everything else all this time, it would be insignificant!

> 若肖久矣，其细也夫！
> Ruò xiào jiǔ yǐ, qí xì yě fū!

If | look like | long time | <!>, | it | tiny/insignificant | <!> | <!>!

Now I have three treasures that I hold and protect:

> 我有三宝持而保之。
> Wǒ yǒu sān bǎo chí ér bǎo zhī.

I | have | three | treasures | grasp/sustain | and | protect | them.

The first is compassion,
The second is frugality,
The third is not daring to be in front.

> 一曰慈，二曰俭，三曰不敢为天下先。
> Yī yuē cí, èr yuē jiǎn, sān yuē bù gǎn wéi tiānxià xiān.

One | called | kind/charitable, |
Two | called | frugal, |
Three | called | not | dare | as | under heaven | first.

Because I'm kind I can be brave.
Because I'm frugal I can be generous.
Because I'm not in front, I can lead others.

> 慈故能勇。俭故能广。不敢为天下先，故能成器长。
> Cí gù néng yǒng. Jiǎn gù néng guǎng. Bù gǎn wéi tiānxià xiān, gù néng chéng qì zhǎng.

Kind/charitable | thus | can | brave. |
Frugal | thus | can | broad/wide. |
Not | dare | as | under heaven | first, | thus | can | become | all things | leader.

Today, people abandon kindness, trying to be brave.
Abandon frugality, trying to be generous.
Abandon following, trying to be in front.
This is death!

> 今舍慈且勇。舍俭且广。舍后且先。死矣！
> Jīn shě cí qiě yǒng. Shě jiǎn qiě guǎng. Shě hòu qiě xiān. Sǐ yǐ!

Now | give up | kind/charitable | take | brave. |
Give up | frugal | take | broad/wide. |
Give up | behind | take | in front. |
Death | <!>!

Kindness in battle brings victory, in defense it brings strength.

> 夫慈以战则胜，以守则固。
> Fū cí yǐ zhàn zé shèng, yǐ shǒu zé gù.

So | kind/charitable | used for | war | then | victory, | used for | defend | then | strong/stable.

Heaven will rescue you,
And with kindness protect you.

> 天将救之，以慈卫之。
> Tiān jiāng jiù zhī, yǐ cí wèi zhī.

Heaven | will | rescue | it, |
With | kind/charitable | guard/defend | it.

68

A good commander is not fierce.
A good warrior is not angry.
A good conqueror doesn't engage the enemy.
A good leader serves from below.

This is called the De of not striving.
This is called the power of leadership.

This is called matching Heaven's ancient way.

A good commander is not fierce.

> 善为士者不武。
> Shànwéi shì zhě bù wǔ.

Good at | military officer/scholar-official | he/she who is | no | attributes of a good soldier.

▶ 武 (wǔ): the attributes of a good soldier: *powerful/formidable in war, valiant, fierce, moral principles to be honored during warfare*

A good warrior is not angry.

> 善战者不怒。
> Shàn zhàn zhě bú nù.

Good | battle | he/she who is | no | anger.

A good conqueror doesn't engage the enemy.

> 善胜敌者不与。
> Shàn shèng dí zhě bù yǔ.

Good | victory | foe | he/she who is | not | engage.

▶ A good conqueror does not get tangled up with the enemy, but stays emotionally calm.

A good leader serves from below.

> 善用人者为之下。
> Shàn yòng rén zhě wéi zhī xià.

Good | use | person | he/she who is | serve | them | below/underneath.

This is called the De of not striving,
This is called the power of leadership.

> 是谓不争之德，是谓用人之力。
> Shì wèi bù zhēng zhī dé, shì wèi yòng rén zhī lì.

Is | called | not | strive/argue | of 之 | De, |
Is | called | use | people | of 之 | power.

▶ 争 (zhēng): *doing whatever you can in order to win*, fight, dispute, contend, strive, struggle

This is called matching Heaven's ancient way.

> 是谓配天古之极。
> Shì wèi pèi tiān gǔ zhī jí.

Is | called | match/fit | heaven | old | of 之 | extreme/final.

69

The masters of war have a saying:
I dare not act like the host, but instead act like a guest.
I dare not advance an inch, but instead retreat a foot.

This is called advancing without advancing,
Striking without using your arms,
Attacking without enemies,
Defending without soldiers.

Nothing is worse than underestimating the enemy.
Underestimating the enemy, I nearly lost my treasures.

So, when opposing armies come together,
The merciful side will be victorious!

The masters of war have a saying:
I dare not act like the host, but instead act like a guest.

> 用兵有言：吾不敢为主，而为客。
> Yòngbīng yǒu yán: Wú bù gǎn wéi zhǔ, ér wéi kè.

One who uses war/weapons | has | saying: |
I/we | not | dare | as | host, | but | as | guest.

▸ In military terms: "I don't dare start a war, I prefer to be the one who defends."

I dare not advance an inch, but instead retreat a foot.

> 不敢进寸，而退尺。
> Bù gǎn jìn cùn, ér tuì chǐ.

Not | dare | advance | inch, | but | retreat | foot.

▸ 寸 (cùn): *a Chinese inch*, the width of a person's thumb at the knuckle. Ten 寸 equal one 尺 (chǐ), a Chinese foot, which is about 9½ inches.

This is called advancing without advancing,
Striking without using your arms,

> 是谓行无行，攘无臂，
> Shì wèi xíng wú xíng, rǎng wú bì,

Is | called | proceed | without | proceeding, |
Strike/stretch out | without | arm,

▸ 行 (xíng): *walk, move, advance forward, go on patrol, move in a circular motion.* So, 行无行 (xíng wú xíng) is literally "walk without walking" or "go without going."

Attacking without enemies,
Defending without soldiers.

> 扔无敌，执无兵。
> Rēng wú dí, zhí wú bīng.

Throw/cast aside | without | foe, |
Hold in hand | without | weapons/soldiers.

▶ 执 (zhí): to *hold*, so in this context, *maintain position, hold the fort*

▶ 兵 (bīng): *soldiers, weapons, warfare* or *military*, depending on context, so it can be read as "defending without warfare"

Nothing is worse than underestimating the enemy.
Underestimating the enemy, I nearly lost my treasures.

> 祸莫大于轻敌。轻敌几丧吾宝。
> Huò mò dà yú qīng dí. Qīng dí jī sàng wú bǎo.

Misfortune | not | large | compared to | underestimate | enemy. |
Underestimate | enemy | almost | lose | my | treasure.

▶ This might refer to the three treasures in Chapter 67.

So, when opposing armies come together,
The merciful side will be victorious!

> 故抗兵相加，哀者胜矣。
> Gù kàng bīng xiāng jiā, āi zhě shèng yǐ.

So | oppose | weapons/soldiers | together | add/meet, |
Merciful/sad | he/she | victory | <!>.

▶ The last line can be read two completely different ways, depending on how one interprets 哀 (āi). If it's *sad*, then the line reads "Only the mourners will be victorious," echoing "victory in war should be treated like a funeral ceremony." in Chapter 31. If it's *pity* or *mercy*, then the line reads as shown above.

70

My words are very easy to understand,
Very easy to practice.

In this world they can't be understood,
And can't be practiced.

My words have ancestors,
My duties have rulers.

So because people don't understand,
They think I don't understand.

Few people understand me.
They are very valuable!

So, the sage wears rough clothing
But carries jade in his heart.

My words are very easy to understand,
Very easy to practice.

> 吾言甚易知，甚易行。
> Wú yán shèn yì zhī, shèn yì xíng.

I | speak/words | very | easy | understand, | very | easy | do.

In this world they can't be understood,
And can't be practiced.

> 天下莫能知，莫能行。
> Tiānxià mò néng zhī, mò néng xíng.

Under heaven | not | can | understand, | not | can | do.

▶ The word 知 (zhī) appears five times in this chapter. It can be a verb meaning *know, understand, perceive, recognize*; or a noun meaning *knowledge, understanding*.

My words have ancestors,
My duties have rulers.

> 言有宗，事有君。
> Yán yǒu zōng, shì yǒu jūn.

Speak/words | have | lineage/ancestry, |
Things/matters | have | ruler/son of heaven.

▶ These lines are very compact and we give a compact translation, however, a more verbose version would be, "My words are guided by an ancient line of teachers, and my duties have been passed down from the Son of Heaven."

So because people don't understand,
They think I don't understand.

> 夫唯无知，是以不我知。
> Fū wéi wú zhī, shìyǐ bù wǒ zhī.

So | although/because/only | not | knowledge, |
Therefore | not | I | knowledge.

▶ There's no pronoun in the first line, but inserting "they" referring to "people" makes the most sense in light of the rest of the chapter. Other possible meanings: "Because they have no knowledge, I am not understood," and "Because I have no knowledge, I don't know anything."

Few people understand me.
They are very valuable!

> 知我者希。则我者贵。
> Zhī wǒ zhě xī. Zé wǒ zhě guì.

Know | me/my | he/she who is | rare. |
Therefore | my | people | valuable.

So, the sage wears rough clothing
But carries jade in his heart.

> 是以圣人被褐怀玉。
> Shìyǐ shèngrén pī hè huái yù.

Therefore | sage | cover/wear | coarse woolen cloth |
Carry in bosom | jade.

▶ 褐 (hè): *a cloth made of coarse fiber*, like a "hair shirt." Also, by extension, *poor* or *ragged*.

71

Knowing that you are ignorant is best,
Being ignorant but thinking that you know is a sickness.

Only when you see sickness as sickness,
Can you be healthy.

The sage is healthy
Because he knows sickness as sickness,
Therefore he is healthy.

Knowing that you are ignorant is best,
Being ignorant but thinking that you know is a sickness.

> 知不知上，不知知病。
> Zhī bùzhī shàng, bùzhī zhī bìng.

Know/knowledge | no knowledge | top/superior, |
No knowledge | know/knowledge | sick(ness).

▶ This chapter is extremely, almost comically concise, and doesn't lend itself to an accurate word-for-word translation. There are almost no pronouns or prepositions or other helpful words in the text, so the meaning is elusive and open to interpretation. The important words to understand are:

- 知 (zhī): *knowledge, understanding, wisdom,* can be a verb, adjective or noun. Used here as a noun: *knowledge of Dao.*

- The opposite of 知 (zhī) is 不知 (bùzhī), *ignorance.*

- 病 (bìng): *sickness, suffering,* and can also be an adjective or a noun. Used here as a noun: *suffering that results from not following Dao.*

- The opposite of 病 (bìng) is 不病 (bú bìng): *health.*

Only when you see sickness as sickness,
Can you be healthy.

> 夫唯病病，是以不病。
> Fū wéi bìng bìng, shìyǐ bú bìng.

So | only | sick(ness) | sick(ness), |
Therefore | not | sick(ness).

▶ In Chinese, doubling a word usually serves to emphasize that word, so 病病 would mean "very sick." But not here; this sentence follows the structure of others in this chapter, so it means "sickness as sickness."

The sage is healthy
Because he knows sickness as sickness,
Therefore he is healthy.

> 圣人不病以其病病，是以不病。
> Shèngrén bú bìng, yǐ qí bìng bìng, shìyǐ bú bìng.

Sage | not | sick(ness) |
Because | he | sick(ness) | sick(ness), |
Therefore | not | sick(ness).

▶ There's no verb in the second line "because he sick sick." We add "knows" because it makes the most sense.

72

If the citizens don't respect power,
Then a greater power will arrive!

Don't disrupt their homes,
Don't despise their lives.

Don't despise them,
And they won't despise you.

Thus the sage
Knows himself but doesn't show off,
Loves himself but isn't arrogant,
Leaves that and chooses this.

If the citizens don't respect power,
Then a greater power will arrive!

> 民不畏威，则大威至。
> Mín bú wèi wēi, zé dà wēi zhì.

Citizens | not | fear/respect | power, |
<!> | great | power | arrive.

Don't disrupt their homes,
Don't despise their lives.

> 无狎其所居，无厌其所生。
> Wú xiá qí suǒ jū, wú yàn qí suǒ shēng.

Not | repress/squeeze | their | of | dwell, |
Not | dislike/detest | their | of | life/birth.

Don't despise them,
And they won't despise you.

> 夫唯不厌，是以不厌。
> Fū wéi bú yàn, shìyǐ bú yàn.

So | only | not | dislike/detest, |
Therefore | not | dislike/detest.

Thus the sage
Knows himself but doesn't show off,
Loves himself but isn't arrogant,

> 是以圣人自知不自见，自爱不自贵，
> Shìyǐ shèngrén zì zhī bú zì xiàn, zì ài bú zì guì,

Therefore | sage |
Oneself | know | not | oneself | see/show, |
Oneself | love | not | oneself | high/valuable,

Leaves that and chooses this.

> 故去彼取此。
> Gù qù bǐ qǔ cǐ.

Thus | give up | that | choose | this.

73

Courage in daring brings death,
Courage in not daring brings life.
Of these two, one is helpful and the other harmful.

When heaven brings failure, who knows its reasons?

The Dao of heaven doesn't strive, but skillfully wins,
Doesn't speak, but skillfully answers,
Doesn't call, but comes itself,
Doesn't hurry, but skillfully prepares.

Heaven's net is extremely vast,
Its mesh is wide but it doesn't fail.

Courage in daring brings death,
Courage in not daring brings life.

> 勇于敢则杀，勇于不敢则活。
> Yǒngyú gǎn zé shā, yǒngyú bù gǎn zé huó.

Courage | daring | <!> | die, |
Courage | not | dare | <!> | live.

Of these two, one is helpful and the other harmful.

> 此两者，或利或害。
> Cǐ liǎng zhě, huò lì huò hài.

These | two | that which is, | some | favorable | some | injury.

When heaven brings failure, who knows its reasons?

> 天之所恶，孰知其故？
> Tiān zhī suǒ wù, shú zhī qí gù?

Heaven | of⇆ | <noun> | harm/evil, | who | understands | its | cause?

▶ Literally, this reads "Things which heaven detests, who knows the cause?" In Laozi's time, heaven was considered the cause of things succeeding or failing, so things fail because of heaven's dislike for them. A modern way to read this is simply, "Who knows why things fail?"

The Dao of heaven doesn't strive, but skillfully wins,

> 天之道，不争而善胜，
> Tiān zhī dào, bù zhēng ér shàn shèng,

Heaven | of⇆ | Dao, | not | strive | but | skillfully | victory,

▶ 善 (shàn): as a noun: *good, kind, virtuous*. As a verb: *expertly, skillfully, successfully, good at*.

Doesn't speak, but skillfully answers,
Doesn't call, but comes itself,
Doesn't hurry, but skillfully prepares.

> 不言而善应，不召而自来，繟然而善谋。
> Bù yán ér shàn yìng, bú zhào ér zì lái, chǎnrán ér shàn móu.

Not | speak | yet | skillfully | respond, |
Not | summon | yet | self | come, |
Calmly | but | skillfully | plan.

▶ 繟 (chǎn): an ancient Chinese word meaning *calm, unhurried*

Heaven's net is extremely vast,
Its mesh is wide but it doesn't fail.

> 天网恢恢，疏而不失。
> Tiān wǎng huīhuī, shū ér bù shī.

Heaven | net | extremely vast, |
Sparse/scattered | but | not | miss/lose.

74

If citizens don't fear death,
Why threaten them with death?

If I could make citizens fear death,
Then I could seize those who act strange and kill them,
And then who would dare?

There will always be an executioner.

The executioner is like a master carpenter carving wood.
One who takes the place of a master carpenter to carve wood,
Won't escape cutting their own hands!

If citizens don't fear death,
Why threaten them with death?

> 民不畏死，奈何以死惧之？
> Mín bú wèi sǐ, nàihé yǐ sǐ jù zhī?

Citizens | not | fear | death, |
But what/who/how/why | use | death | fear | them?

▶ The "if" isn't explicit in this version of the Chinese text, but it appears in others.

▶ This chapter advises rulers on how to use force in society. To summarize the entire chapter: "If capital punishment is applied randomly or unfairly, it's not an effective deterrent to crime and it injures the one who does it. But if used skillfully it works, just like how a master carpenter carves wood."

If I could make citizens fear death,

> 若使民常畏死，
> Ruò shǐ mín cháng wèi sǐ,

If | cause | citizens | frequent/common | fear | death,

Then I could seize those who act strange and kill them,

> 而为奇者吾得执而杀之，
> Ér wéi qí zhě wú dé zhí ér shā zhī,

Then | be | strange | one who is | I | get | hold | then | kill | them,

▶ 奇 (qí) as an adjective: *odd, curious, queer, strange, outstanding.* Interesting that Laozi doesn't simply say "seize those who do wrong" or "commit crimes."

And then who would dare?

> 孰敢?
> Shú gǎn?

Who | dares?

There will always be an executioner.

> 常有司杀者杀。
> Cháng yǒu sī shāzhě shā.

Common/frequent | have | take charge | executioner | kill.

The executioner is like a master carpenter carving wood.

> 夫司杀者是大匠斲。
> Fū sī shāzhě shì dà jiàng zhuó.

So | take charge | executioner | is | great | craftsman | cut/chop.

One who takes the place of a master carpenter to carve wood,
Won't escape cutting their own hands!

> 夫代大匠斲者，希有不伤其手矣。
> Fū dài dà jiàng zhuó zhě, xī yǒu bù shāng qí shǒu yǐ.

So | replace | great | craftsman | cut/chop | that person, |
Rarely | have | not | wound | his | hand | <!>.

75

The citizens are hungry,
Because their superiors take too much of their food.
That's why they are hungry.

The citizens are hard to rule,
Because their superiors are compelled to act.
That's why they are hard to rule.

The citizens take death lightly,
Because their superiors pursue the rich things in life.
Thus they take death lightly.

Thus, those who act without concern for life,
Are worth more than those who highly value life.

The citizens are hungry,
Because their superiors take too much of their food.
That's why they are hungry.

> 民之饥，以其上食税之多。是以饥。
> Mín zhī jī, yǐ qí shàng shí shuì zhī duō. Shìyǐ jī.

Citizens | of⇆ | hungry, |
Because | their | high/superior | food | taxes | of⇆ | much. |
Therefore | hungry.

▶ At the time this was written, taxes were taken in grain.

The citizens are hard to rule,
Because their superiors are compelled to act.
That's why they are hard to rule.

> 民之难治，以其上之有为。是以难治。
> Mín zhī nán zhì, yǐ qí shàng zhī yǒu wéi. Shìyǐ nán zhì.

Citizens | of⇆ | difficult | govern, |
Because | their | high | of⇆ | has | act. |
Therefore | difficult | govern.

▶ The ideal ruler follows 为无为 (wéi wúwéi), acting without acting. The rulers in this chapter are the opposite, they are greedy and act through compulsion.

The citizens take death lightly,
Because their superiors pursue the rich things in life.
Thus they take death lightly.

> 民之轻死，以其求生之厚。是以轻死。
> Mín zhī qīng sǐ, yǐ qí qiú shēng zhī hòu. Shìyǐ qīng sǐ.

Citizens | of之 | light/small | death, |
Because | their | seek | life | of之 | thick/deep/rich. |
Therefore | light/small | death.

Thus, those who act without concern for life,
Are worth more than those who highly value life.

> 夫唯无以生为者，是贤于贵生。
> Fū wéi wú yǐ shēng wéi zhě, shì xián yú guì shēng.

So | only | without | take | life | as | that which is, |
Are | virtuous | in | high/valuable | life.

76

People are born soft and weak,
They die hard and strong.

All creatures, grass and trees are born soft and fragile,
They die dry and withered.

Hard and strong are disciples of death,
Soft and weak are disciples of life.

An unyielding army is defeated,
An unbending tree is ready to fall.

Big and strong dwell below,
Soft and flexible dwell above.

People are born soft and weak,
They die hard and strong.

> 人之生也柔弱，其死也坚强。
> Rén zhī shēng yě róu ruò, qí sǐ yě jiān qiáng.

People | of 之 | born | <!> | soft/gentle | weak/fragile, |
They | die | <!> | hard/strong | powerful.

All creatures, grass and trees are born soft and fragile,
They die dry and withered.

> 万物草木之生也柔脆，其死也枯槁。
> Wànwù cǎo mù zhī shēng yě róu cuì, qí sǐ yě kūgǎo.

Ten thousand things/creatures | grass | trees | of 之 | life/birth | <!> | soft/gentle | fragile, |
They | die | <!> | withered/decayed.

Hard and strong are disciples of death,
Soft and weak are disciples of life.

> 故坚强者死之徒，柔弱者生之徒。
> Gù jiānqiáng zhě sǐ zhī tú, róu ruò zhě shēng zhī tú.

So | strong | he/she who is | die | of 之 | follow, soft/gentle |
Weak/fragile | that which is | birth/life | of 之 | follow.

▶ There's not a good English word for 徒 (tú). It could be *follows, obeys, is a disciple of, travels in the company of*.

An unyielding army is defeated,
An unbending tree is ready to fall.

> 是以兵强则不胜，木强则共。
> Shìyǐ bīng qiáng zé bú shèng, mù qiáng zé gòng.

Therefore | weapon/soldier | strong | <!> | no | victory, |
Wood/tree | strong | <!> | together.

▶ Because 兵 (bīng) can also mean *weapon*, the line could read, "a stiff weapon is easily broken."

Big and strong dwell below,
Soft and flexible dwell above.

> 强大处下，柔弱处上。
> Qiáng dà chǔ xià, róu ruò chǔ shàng.

Strong | great | dwell | under, |
Soft/gentle | weak/fragile | dwell | on top.

▶ Some say this refers to the structure of a tree – the strong but stiff trunk below, and the soft flexible branches above. But more likely it refers to people, where inflexible people (yang) are inferior but flexible people (yin) are superior. As we've seen, soft and yielding overcomes strong and hard.

77

The Dao of heaven, how it is like bending a bow?

That which is high, press it down.
That which is low, raise it up.

That which has too much, take away.
That which has not enough, add more.

The Dao of heaven
Reduces that which has too much,
Fills that which has too little.

The way of people isn't like this,
It takes from that which has too little,
And offers it to that which has too much.

Who can have too much and then offer it to the world?
Only one who has Dao.

Thus the sage
Acts but does not compel,
Accomplishes tasks but doesn't dwell on them,
And has no desire to show off worth.

The Dao of heaven, how it is like bending a bow?

> 天之道，其犹张弓与？
> Tiān zhī dào, qí yóu zhāng gōng yǔ?

Heaven | of 与 | Dao, | its | compared to | stretch | bow | <!>?

▶ It's tempting to read the next nine lines as referring to people, for example "Those who are high, it brings down." But nothing in the text actually refers to people. There are no pronouns at all, only 者 (zhě), which means "that which is," as in, "that which is high." This ties in nicely with the first line, which compares the action of Dao to something impersonal, the bending of a bow.

That which is high, press it down.
That which is low, raise it up.

> 高者，抑之。下者，举之。
> Gāo zhě, yì zhī. Xià zhě, jǔ zhī.

High | that which is, | press down | it. |
Below | that which is, | raise | it.

That which has too much, take away.
That which has not enough, add more.

> 有余者，损之。不足者，补之。
> Yǒu yú zhě, sǔn zhī. Bù zú zhě, bǔ zhī.

Have | surplus | that which is, | diminish | it. |
Not | enough | that which is, | supplement | it.

The Dao of heaven
Reduces that which has too much,
Fills that which has too little.

> 天之道损有余，而补不足。
> Tiān zhī dào sǔn yǒuyú, ér bǔ bùzú.

Heaven | of⇆ | Dao |
Diminish | have surplus, |
Yet | supplement | not enough/sufficient.

The way of people isn't like this,
It takes from that which has too little,
And offers it to that which has too much.

> 人之道，则不然，损不足以奉有余。
> Rén zhī dào, zé bù rán, sǔn bùzú yǐ fèng yǒuyú.

People | of⇆ | way, | <!> | not | such, |
Diminish | insufficient, |
In order to | offer/receive | have surplus.

▸ Here 道 (dào) is not Dao, but *way* or *path* of people, in contrast to the Dao of heaven.

Who can have too much and then offer it to the world?
Only one who has Dao.

> 孰能有余以奉天下，唯有道者。
> Shú néng yǒu yú yǐ fèng tiānxià, wéi yǒu dào zhě.

Who | can | have | surplus | thus | offer/receive | under heaven, |
Only | have | Dao | that which is.

Thus the sage
Acts but does not compel,

> 是以圣人为而不恃，
> Shìyǐ shèngrén wéi ér bú shì,

Therefore | sage |
Make | yet | not | rely on,

Accomplishes tasks but doesn't dwell on them,
And has no desire to show off worth.

> 功成而不处，其不欲见贤。
> Gōng chéng ér bù chǔ, qí bú yù jiàn xián.

Accomplish | completed | yet | not | remain, |
He | not | desires | show | virtue/value.

78

In this world nothing is softer and weaker than water,
Yet for attacking that which is hard and strong,
Nothing can surpass it,
Nothing can replace it.

Weak is better than strong,
Flexible is better than hard.

In this world,
None fails to comprehend this,
None can practice it.

Thus the sage says:
Taking on the dirt of the nation
Is called being the master of the altars of field and grains.
Taking on the misfortune of the nation
Is called being king of the world.

Straight talk may seem contrary.

In this world nothing is softer and weaker than water,

> 天下莫柔弱于水，
> Tiānxià mò róu ruò yú shuǐ,
>
> Under heaven | no | soft/pliant | weak/fragile | than | water,

Yet for attacking that which is hard and strong,
Nothing can surpass it,
Nothing can replace it.

> 而攻坚强者，莫之能胜，其无以易之。
> Ér gong jiān qiáng zhě, mò zhī néng shēng, qí wú yǐ yì zhī.
>
> Yet | attack | hard | strong | that which is, |
> Not | it | can | victorious, |
> There is | nothing | with which | exchange | it.

Weak is better than strong,
Flexible is better than hard.

> 弱之胜强，柔之胜刚。
> Ruò zhī shèng qiáng, róu zhī shèng gāng,
>
> Weak/fragile | it | surpass/get the better of | strong, |
> Soft/pliant | it | surpass/get the better of | hard/tough.

In this world,
None fails to comprehend this,
None can practice it.

> 天下，莫不知，莫能行。
> Tiānxià, mò bù zhī, mò néng xíng.

Under heaven, |
Not | no | understand, |
Not | can | do.

Thus the sage says:
Taking on the dirt of the nation
Is called being the master of the altars of field and grains.

> 是以圣人云：受国之垢，是谓社稷主。
> Shìyǐ shèngrén yún: Shòu guó zhī gòu, shì wèi shè jì zhǔ.

Therefore | sage | says: |
Receive | nation | of 与 | dirt, |
Is | called | god of soil | god of grains | lord.

▶ 国之垢 (guózhī gòu): *dirt of the nation*, but more accurately, the humiliation or disgrace of the nation.

▶ 社 (shè): *the altar of the god of earth, land, soil.* 稷 (jì): *the altar of the god of grain and crops.* These according to Roberts[1] refer to the ruler of a kingdom, however, kingdoms were relatively small during the Warring States period when Laozi lived. This contrasts with "king of the world" or "king under heaven" in the next line which refers to the ruler of the Zhou court, which at one time (several centuries before Laozi) was the universal sovereign for all of China.

Taking on the misfortune of the nation
Is called being king of the world.

> 受国不祥是谓天下王。
> Shòu guó bùxiáng shì wèi tiānxià wáng.

---

[1] Roberts, Moss: *Dao de Jing: The Book of the Way*, University of California Press, 2001.

Receive | nation | bad fortune |
Is | called | under heaven | king.

Straight talk may seem contrary.

> 正言若反。
> Zhèngyán ruò fǎn.

Straight talk | same as | opposite/turned around.

▶ Yes, it certainly seems that way...

79

Reconcile a great grievance,
And there will certainly be lingering grievances.
How can this be good?

Thus the sage
Holds the left side of a contract,
But makes no demands of people.

Having De, look after your obligations,
Without De, look after your claims on others.

The Dao of heaven has no favorites,
But it always favors sincere people.

Reconcile a great grievance,
And there will certainly be lingering grievances.

> 和大怨，必有余怨。
> Hé dà yuàn, bì yǒu yú yuàn.

Harmony/peace | great | hatred, |
Certainly | have | leftover/lingering | hatred.

▶ 怨 (yuàn): *hatred, grievance arising from a dispute.*

How can this be good?

> 安可以为善？
> Ān kěyǐ wéi shàn?

How | can | make | good?

Thus the sage
Holds the left side of a contract,
But makes no demands of people.

> 是以圣人执左契，而不责于人。
> Shìyǐ shèngrén zhí zuǒ qì, ér bù zé yú rén.

Therefore | sage |
Hold in hand | left | contract, |
Yet | not | demand/require | from | people.

▶ In ancient China, a contract was carved on two pieces of board. The left portion was for the lender, the right portion for the borrower.

Having De, look after your obligations,
Without De, look after your claims on others.

> 有德，司契，无德，司彻。
> Yǒu dé, sī qì, wú dé, sī chè.

Have | De, | manage | contract, |
Not have | De, | manage | claim/tax.

▶ 司 (sī): *manage, look after, control, see to, take charge of*

The Dao of heaven has no favorites,
But it always favors sincere people.

> 天道无亲，常与善人。
> Tiān dào wú qīn, cháng yǔ shàn rén.

Heaven | Dao | without | favorite/ally, |
Always | supports/favors | good/sincere | people.

80

A small nation with few citizens,
Has the weapons of a hundred men,
But doesn't use them.

The citizens take death seriously, but they don't travel far.
They have boats and carts, but they don't need to ride them.
They have armor and weapons, but they don't need to display them.

Let the citizens return to using knotted cords,
Finding sweetness in their food,
Beauty in their clothes,
Contentment in their homes,
Enjoyment in their traditions.

Other nations can be seen nearby,
Sounds of chickens and dogs can be heard,
But the citizens reach old age and die,
Without traveling far to visit each other.

A small nation with few citizens,
Has the weapons of a hundred men,
But doesn't use them.

> 小国寡民，使有仕百人之器，而不用。
> Xiǎo guó guǎ mín, shǐ yǒu shì bǎi rén zhī qì, ér búyòng.

Small | nation | few | citizens, |
Even though | have | official | hundred | people | of ⇆ | instrument, |
Yet | don't use.

The citizens take death seriously, but they don't travel far.

> 使民重死，而不远徙。
> Shǐ mín zhòng sǐ, ér bù yuǎn xǐ.

Even though | citizens | heavy/important | die, | yet | not | far | move.

They have boats and carts, but they don't need to ride them.

> 虽有舟舆，无所乘之。
> Suī yǒu zhōu yú, wú suǒ chéng zhī.

Though | have | boats | carts, | not | about | ride | it.

They have armor and weapons, but they don't need to display them.

> 虽有甲兵，无所陈之。
> Suī yǒu jiǎ bīng, wú suǒ chén zhī.

Though | have | armor | soldiers, | not | about | display | it.

Let the citizens return to using knotted cords,
Finding sweetness in their food,

> 使民复结绳而用之，甘其食，
> Shǐ mín fù jié shéng ér yòng zhī, gān qí shí,

Let | citizens | return | tie | rope | and | use | them, |
Sweet | their | food,

▶ Before China had written characters, intricate knotted cords were used to sign contracts and store information.

Beauty in their clothes,
Contentment in their homes,
Enjoyment in their traditions.

> 美其服，安其居，乐其俗。
> Měi qí fú, ān qí jū, lè qí sú.

Beautiful | their | clothes, |
Stable/peaceful | their | dwellings, |
Musical/happy | their | habits/traditions.

Other nations can be seen nearby,
Sounds of chickens and dogs can be heard,

> 邻国相望，鸡犬之声相闻，
> Lín guó xiāng wàng, jī quǎn zhī shēng xiāng wén,

Neighbor | nations | together | look at/look forward, |
Chicken | dog | of⇆ | sound | together | hear,

But the citizens reach old age and die,
Without traveling far to visit each other.

> 民至老死，不相往来。
> Mín zhì lǎo sǐ, bù xiāng wǎnglái.

Citizens | reach | old | die, |
Not | each other | going and coming.

▶ The last line is, literally, "Without coming and going to visit each other."

81

True words aren't pretty,
Pretty words aren't true.

One who is good doesn't argue,
One who argues isn't good.

One who knows doesn't boast,
One who boasts doesn't know.

The sage doesn't accumulate,
But by serving people, gains even more.
By giving to people, has even more.

The Dao of heaven transforms but doesn't harm.
The Dao of the sage acts but doesn't strive.

True words are not pretty,
Pretty words are not true.

> 信言不美，美言不信。
> Xìn yán bù měi, měi yán bú xìn.

True | words | not | beautiful/pleasing, |
Beautiful/pleasing | words | not | true.

▶ 美 (měi): often translated as *beautiful*, but it has an undercurrent of *attractive in order to please others*.

One who is good doesn't argue,
One who argues isn't good.

> 善者不辩，辩者不善。
> Shàn zhě bú biàn, biàn zhě bú shàn.

Good | he who has | not | debate, |
Debate | he who has | not | good.

▶ 辩 (biàn): *argue*, but in the sense of *use clever words in scholarly debate,* not in the sense of an argument or shouting match.

One who knows doesn't boast,
One who boasts doesn't know.

> 知者不博，博者不知。
> Zhì zhě bù bó, bó zhě bù zhī.

Know | he who has | not | abundant, |
Abundance | he who has | not | know.

▶ 博 (bó): originally, *ten sellers of silk loudly promoting their wares at a marketplace,* in other words, one who makes loud announcements. Later the word evolved to mean *taking risks in hope of a favorable outcome, to gamble,* and still later, *abundant, plentiful.*

The sage doesn't accumulate,
But by serving people, gains even more.

> 圣人不积，既以为人己愈有。
> Shèngrén bù jī, jì yǐ wéi rén jǐ yù yǒu.

Sage | not | accumulate, |
Already | give | for | people | self | even more | have.

By giving to people, has even more.

> 既以与人，己愈多。
> Jì yǐ yǔ rén, jǐ yù duō.

Already | give | for | people, | self | even more | more.

The Dao of heaven transforms but doesn't harm.

> 天之道利而不害。
> Tiān zhī dào, lì ér bú hài.

Heaven | of⇆ | Dao | benefit | yet | not | injure.

▶ 利 (lì): some translate this as *benefit*, but the word has an undercurrent of sharpness to it. The origin of this word is *to clear ground for cultivation*.

The Dao of the sage acts but doesn't strive.

> 圣人之道为而不争。
> Shèngrén zhī dào wéi ér bù zhēng.

Sage | of⇆ | Dao | help | yet | not | strive.

Translation Notes

There are hundreds of translations of the Dao De Jing[2], which we'll abbreviate as DDJ from here on. They all follow a similar format: they begin with detailed notes written by the translator that discuss the book, its underlying philosophy, and the translation process, and that's followed by the translated text itself. As you see, we've taken the opposite approach: the DDJ comes first, and here at the end we'll just give you some brief notes.

When we say "brief" we're not kidding. We'll start off with a little bit of history of the DDJ itself, then talk about how we approached this translation project, and give you some tips on how you can best use this book.

However, if you're looking for a detailed discussion on Daoism, you'll have to look elsewhere. There are many excellent books on Daoism, some of which are listed in the Resources section, but we prefer not to talk very much about that. Our single goal is to give you the DDJ, the whole DDJ, and nothing but the DDJ, in a clear style that's as close as possible to the original, and let you decide for yourself what the words mean.

People have spent over two thousand years trying to understand and interpret the DDJ. Now it's your turn to read the book and come up with your own understanding of its timeless wisdom.

道

Nobody really knows who wrote the DDJ.

A popular folk tale tells how it might have happened. A long time ago, China was not a unified country but just a patchwork of small feudal kingdoms

---

[2] You may have seen this book called the *Tao Te Ching* or *Tao Teh Ching*. That was the name of the book in English until 1958, when the Chinese government replaced the old Wade-Giles sysem of romanizing Chinese proper names with new names that used pinyin spelling and correct pronounciation. So, for example, Peking became Beijing, and Mao Tse Tung became Mao Zedong, Tao became Dao, Taoism became Daoism, and the Tao Te Ching became the Dao De Jing.

constantly at war with each other. The people longed for a return to peace and order.

In the central plains of China, in the ancient capital city of Chengzhou, lived a man who we know today as Laozi. He was a quiet and learned man who served as a court librarian, hand-copying documents and managing the court's ancient archives. Although he was somewhat reclusive, he attracted many students and disciples and was a respected wise man. This was in the days when Confucius also lived and taught.

One day Confucius went to see Laozi, hoping that the old archivist would share a bit of ancient knowledge and, of course, treat him with respect and deference. Instead, Laozi sharply rebuked Confucius, telling him that his head was too full of rules and regulations and that he would do well to forget all that

Figure 1: stone sculpture of Laozi, at the foot of Mount Qingyuan, Fujian Province, in eastern China.

complexity and simply follow the Dao, the natural way of things. Confucius was stunned. He disappeared for several days, then emerged and told his followers that he had met many impressive people in his life, but none could compare with Laozi, who was "truly like a dragon."

When Laozi was nearing the end of his life, he became tired of the ways of people and decided to head to the western mountains and leave the civilized world for good. But when he reached the western boundary of the Zhou

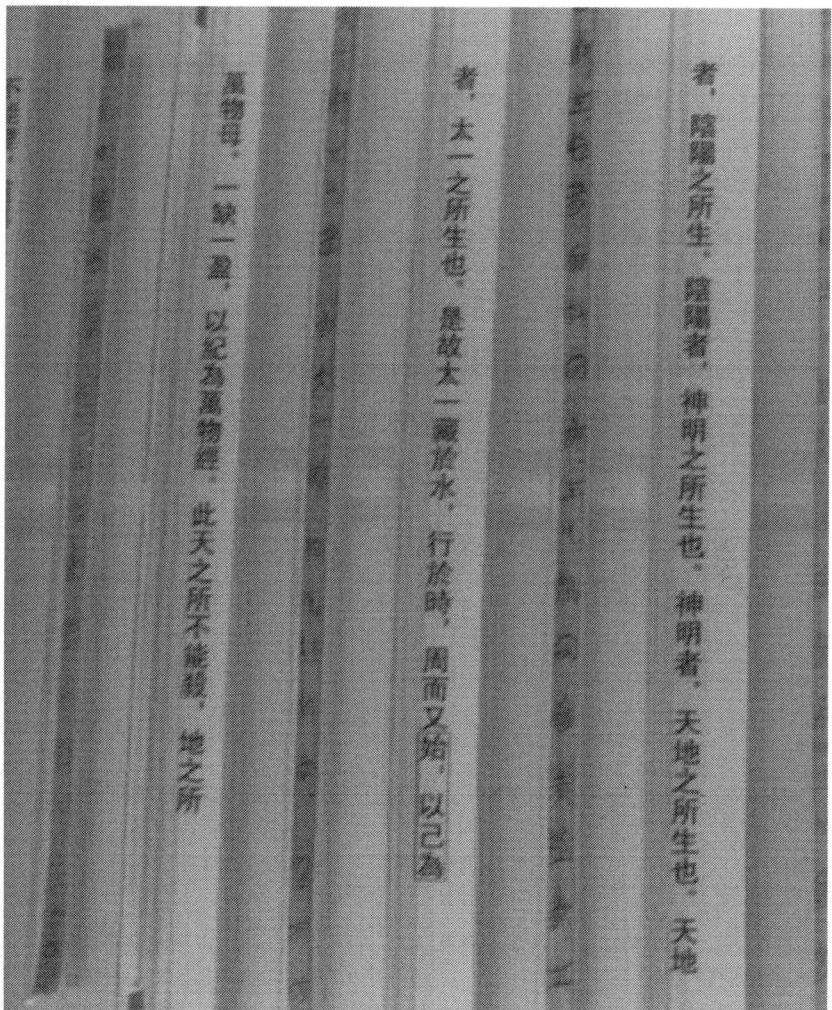

Figure 2: The Guodian Chu Slips, the earliest known Dao De Jing manuscript, written on bamboo slips, with description and explanation alongside, in white. In Hubei Provincial Museum, China.

kingdom, a border guard named Yinxi recognized him, and begged him to record some of his wisdom before disappearing into the wilderness. Laozi agreed, and his writings on strips of bamboo later became known as the DDJ. When he was finished, he continued on his way and was never seen or heard from again.

For centuries, many Daoists have believed that Laozi, also called Lord Lao, was a manifestation of the Dao itself, conceived when his mother gazed upon a falling star. Not surprisingly, they consider the DDJ to be a divinely revealed document. But scholars and historians agree that regardless of who Laozi was or wasn't, the book we know of today as the DDJ was not the work of a single author, but has been modified and enhanced many times over the centuries. Evidence for this is clear from the half-dozen ancient manuscripts that have been discovered in the last hundred years. The oldest known version of the text, the Guodian Chu Slips, was discovered in 1993 (see Figure 2). Found in a tomb near the town of Guodian, it was written on strips of bamboo in the 4th century BCE but only contained 31 of the 81 chapters. Several other versions have been discovered, most notably the Mawangdui manuscript containing all 81 chapters, written on silk and dating from 200 BCE and unearthed in 1973 (see Figure 3).

On the other hand, some versions of the DDJ have been in general circulation ever since they were originally written in the time of Laozi. These texts, called the "received versions," have been hand-copied many times over the centuries, and often include commentaries. The received versions differ from the more recently discovered manuscripts, which all differ from each other. The contents of individual chapters vary from one manuscript to another, the orders of the chapters change (in some versions the Dao section is placed after the De section), and some verses and entire chapters appear and disappear from one manuscript to the next.[3]

---

[3] In this book, our starting point is the "consensus version" developed by Bruce R. Linnell and published online as *Dao De Jing: A Minimalist Translation* (www.gutenberg.org/files/49965/49965-h/49965-h.htm). Linnell started with the three highest quality received versions – Wang Bi, Heshang Gong and Fu Yi – and wherever he encountered disagreement among those sources, he simply used the wording that two of the three sources agreed upon.

Figure 3: Ink on silk manuscript of the Dao De Jing, 2nd century BC, unearthed in 1973 in Mawangdui tomb, Chansha, Hunan Province, China.

The first known English translation of the DDJ was published by Protestant missionary John Chalmers in 1868 and called *The Speculations on Metaphysics, Polity, and Morality of the 'Old Philosopher' Lau-tsze.* Many other translations followed, and today there are said to be over 250 translations into major Western languages. Some try to remain as faithful as possible to the original Chinese text. Others tend to incorporate the translators' own beliefs and cultural biases, adding words and concepts that never existed in the text of the original DDJ.

道

As we designed this book and worked on the translation, we have kept three goals in mind.

First, we want to express the DDJ in simple language that anyone can access. This is a book for ordinary people, not scholars. Many DDJ translations have been created by scholars for other scholars, and while we have studied many of them and owe a debt of gratitude to those scholars, we feel that the DDJ's message is simple, practical and universal, and we want everyone to have the chance to benefit from it. We try to follow the guidance of Laozi in Chapter 70, who tells us, in his usual elliptical way:

> My words are very easy to understand,
> Very easy to practice.
> In this world, they can't be understood,
> And can't be practiced.

Maybe we can't help you put the DDJ's works into practice in your everyday life, but at least we can help you understand Laozi's words.

Second, we want to give you a peek behind the translator's curtain. In our research we could not find a single translation that actually lets the non-Chinese speaking reader make connections between the original text and the final English translation. We've read many translations, but they're just that –

translations. If you read several different translations of the same chapter, you may get a general idea of what the original must have been like, but this tends to be a combination of detective work and guessing, not supported by having access to the original Chinese. We are trying to fix that, *by giving you the tools you need to translate the DDJ for yourself, even if you don't speak any Chinese.*

To accomplish this, we've taken the unusual step of not just giving you the English translation, but also showing, word by word, how one gets from the original Chinese characters to the English version. You'll see this in the translation notes section of each chapter, where you'll see our English translation, followed by a word-by-word and line-by-line breakdown of how we translated the original text.

Here is an example of what you see in the translation notes for each verse in each chapter:

Being present, see the appearance.

常有欲以观其徼。
Cháng yǒu yùyǐ guān qí jiǎo.
Often/usually | have | desire | in order to | see | its | edges.

徼 (jiǎo): *boundary, border, edge.* Being engaged in this world can prevent us from seeing the still depths of the nameless mysteries.

You'll see:

- Our final English translation of the verse.

- The original Chinese verse, written in Simplified characters.

- The same Chinese characters repeated in pinyin. If a word is made up of two characters, like yùyǐ in this example, the pinyin is combined into a single word.

- A word-for-word literal translation. Each pinyin word corresponds to a section in this line, and vertical bars separate them. In this example, 欲以 (yùyǐ) is defined as "in order to." You may notice that the same Chinese word may be translated into different English words. This is because the meaning of Chinese words, like English words, depends on context. For that reason, we show you the meaning of the word in this particular verse.

- Occasional comments as needed to help you better understand the translation.

It's impossible, or at least inadvisable, to do a 100% literal translation of the DDJ. Modern Chinese is different from Western languages, and the language used in this book is even more different. To start with, the DDJ is extremely compact. Its verses have very few connecting words, forcing the reader to think deeply about the verse in order to tease out its underlying meaning or meanings. Some words can, depending on context, serve as nouns, verbs, adjectives or adverbs. Verbs in Chinese generally have no past, present or future tense, nouns have no gender (male/female), and no number (singular/plural). And to make things even more difficult, helpful little words like prepositions and pronouns are often missing entirely.

As a result, translating literally from Chinese to English usually results in gibberish. We've added just enough connecting words so that the sentence makes sense, while still expressing Laozi's thoughts as concisely as possible.

We've also tried really hard to avoid the temptation to add things that weren't already there in order to make the sentence more readable. Whenever we do that (for example, adding a pronoun to a sentence that doesn't have one), we note it in the commentary.

How many ways are there to translate the DDJ? Here's a short example. The first verse of Chapter 23 simply reads 希言自然 [4]. This verse has only three Chinese words, requiring a total of four characters. The first word 希 (xī) means *rare*, 言 (yán) means *speak*, and 自然 (zìrán) means *nature* or *natural*, depending on context. Obviously, "Rare speak nature" or "Rare speak natural" would be terrible English. So, here's how various scholars have translated this three-word verse:

1. Speak little. (Star)
2. Nature's words are few. (our translation)
3. Nature says few words. (Light of Spirit)
4. Infrequent speech is natural. (C. Abbott)
5. To speak little is natural. (Muller)
6. In Nature nothing is eternal. (Flowing Hands)
7. To talk little is natural. (Feng/English)
8. To be of few words is natural. (Stenudd)
9. Nature does not have to insist. (Garafalo)
10. Minimal words are naturally so. (Gutenberg Project)
11. Taciturnity is natural to man. (Goddard)
12. Spare speech and let things be. (Roberts)
13. It is natural to speak only rarely. (Ames/Hall)
14. To be taciturn is the natural way. (Susuki)
15. To be sparse in speech is to be spontaneous. (Eno)
16. To use words but rarely is to be natural. (Lau)
17. Saying no words makes things come about by themselves. (Matsumoto)
18. Less spoken, words speak for themselves naturally. (Wikisource)
19. Abstaining from speech marks him who is obeying the spontaneity of his nature. (Legge)

---

[4] The Chinese characters used in this book are Simplified Chinese; this is the set of characters developed in the 1950's and 1960's by the mainland Chinese government to improve literacy by making it easier to read and write. For example, the traditional character for "book" is 書, which was simplified to 书. The DDJ was written using a set of ancient, regional chacters that evolved over time and were eventually transcribed into seal script, then clerical script, and later into what's known today as Traditional Chinese.

You can see that these nineteen translations give us at least ten completely different meanings for this line! Also, the three original Chinese words have morphed into anywhere from 2 to 13 words of English, and in last three examples, the translators have added words and meaning that were nowhere to be found in the original.

One of the reasons why translators use so many words is that they often try to nail down, with finality, an exact meaning. But the DDJ is full of ambiguous lines. In fact, it seems that Laozi delighted in putting together conflicting or unexpected words, leaving it up to the reader to figure out his meaning. We have no problem with ambiguity. In some cases, we've been able to translate into English while preserving multiple possible meanings. In other cases, we've had to pick one meaning but have noted other possible meanings in the translation notes.

That brings us to our third and final goal: we feel that it's not enough to create a plain English translation; it's just as important to preserve the feeling, the brevity and the rhythm of the original as much as possible. The DDJ's verses are incredibly compact as you've seen from the example above, and they have a rhythmic structure that's often lost or garbled when translated to English. We've tried really hard to preserve those rhythms as much as possible, which sometimes results in English that's not quite grammatically correct but, we hope, captures the essence of the original.

A final note about gender. Chinese is mostly gender-neutral; words are generally not male or female. For example, 人 (rén) means *person* or *people*, not necessarily *man, men, woman* or *women*, and the third-person pronoun 者 (zhě) means *he, she, him, her, them,* or *it*, depending on context. We've maintained this gender neutrality, with just three exceptions. Whenever the word 夫 (fū) is used to mean *men*, this is clearly masculine so we use *men* instead of *people*. When talking about rulers and kings, we use masculine pronouns in keeping with Chinese history. And we use *he, his* or *him* where it would be too awkward (or simply wrong, in the case of Chapter 55) to force the English to be gender neutral.

道

There are Chinese characters throughout this book. How do you read them? Here are a few insights that may be helpful.

Chinese characters represent meaning, not sounds. Here, for example, are some common words, shown in the ancient Oracle Bone Script, as well as their modern versions in Simplified Chinese:

人	男	女	子	夫	妻	王	口
rén	nán	nǚ	zi	fu	qī	wáng	kǒu
person	man	woman	child	husband	wife	king	mouth
目	耳	心	日	月	山	雨	田
mù	ěr	xīn	rì	yuè	shān	yǔ	tián
eye	ear	heart	sun	moon	mountain	rain	field

At one time there was a strong similarity between the appearance of a character and its meaning, but much of that has been lost over time. Looking at a character, you cannot tell what it means, and you cannot tell how to pronounce it. Both must be memorized.[5]

These characters are then combined into sentences, just like in English. But unlike English, Classical Chinese has no word breaks and no punctuation. Most words require just one character, but some require two or even more, and looking at the lines of text, there's no way to tell the difference between a one-character and a multi-character word. And because there's no such thing as

---

[5] This is not completely true; some characters resemble what they stand for, and some have meaning and/or pronounciation hints embedded in them, but these hints aren't enough to reliably sound out words or phrases.

upper or lowercase letters, you can't look at Chinese text and see where a new sentence begins, or when you encounter a proper name.

Here, for example, is the entire text of Chapter 1:

道可道非常道名可名非常名无名天地之始有名万物之母故常无欲以观其妙常有欲以观其徼此两者同出而异名同谓之玄之又玄众妙之门

As you see, there are no spaces between words, and no punctuation at all. The commas, semicolons, dashes, periods and line breaks that you see elsewhere in this book were added later. We include this after-the-fact punctuation in all versions of the text – the Chinese, the pinyin, and the English – because leaving it out would just make it too hard to understand.

In modern Chinese there are also visual breaks between paragraphs and chapters. Not so in the original DDJ manuscripts. Look at the photo of the Mawangdui manuscript in Figure 3. It contains several chapters of the DDJ, but there are no visual clues as to where one chapter ends and another begins.

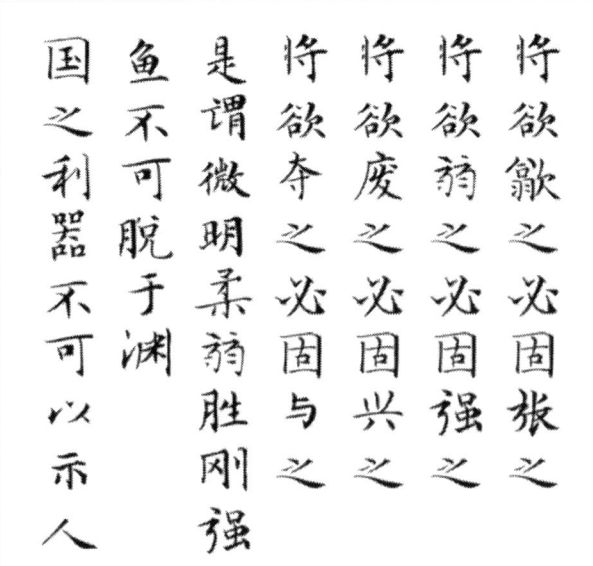

Figure 4: Chapter 36 in Chinese characters. Read each column top-to-bottom and start with the rightmost column. Note the repeating characters in the 1st, 2nd, 4th, 5th, 6th and 8th positions of the first four columns.

Modern Chinese is written left-to-right like English, but the DDJ was originally written on scrolls in vertical columns, each column read top-to-bottom and the columns running from right to left.

So, if there's no way to look at a Chinese character and see to pronounce it, how can you do it without spending years studying the language? To help you with that, we show each character in pinyin, which is a phonetic method of writing Chinese. If for example the character 妈 is written in pinyin as mā, it means "mother" in English.

The tone marks over the vowels are important, because simply saying "ma" like we do in English is ambiguous. Mǎ (with the down-then-up tone ǎ) means *horse*, but the same word spoken with different tones has other meanings. We won't get into too much Chinese pronouciation, but you should know the four basic tones plus the fifth "no tone":

Tone	Sound	Example
1st	High, flat	妈 (mā) means mother
2nd	Rising	麻 (má) means hemp or flax
3rd	Down-then-up	马 (mǎ) means horse
4th	Downward	骂 (mà) means scold or curse
No tone	Very short, flat	吗 (ma) at the end of a sentence indicates a question

The consonants shown in pinyin are not necessarily the same as what they'd be in English. A few are pronounced the same, some are slightly different, and a few are quite different.

Glossary

The following words are used frequently in the DDJ.

百姓 (bǎi xìng): *one hundred surnames, one hundred families*. It refers to the common people.

常 (cháng): has three completely different meanings in the DDJ, depending on context and history. Generally, it means *often* or *common*. Sometimes it's used simply to soften the feeling or impact of a sentence and has no meaning other than that. But in several places in the DDJ, for example the famous first two lines of Chapter 1, 常 (cháng) replaces 恆 (héng) which means *eternal* or *everlasting* but was taboo because it was the name of Emperor Wen of Han, whose personal name was Liu Heng. Because of this taboo, scribes replaced 恆 with 常, but we use the meaning of the original 恆 in our translation.

德 (dé): *morality, virtue, living in harmony with dào*. In early times, the character dé depicted a picture of a figure standing on an astronomical observatory center with eyes observing the movement of the sun and stars. Later, the meaning of dé evolved to mean keeping one's eyes on the road ahead, staying in line with nature, and conforming the laws of nature, mankind and society. Laozi used the term dé to describe the way that one behaves when in harmony with dào. So if dào is the way of everything in nature, then dé is the way that everything manifests.

道 (dào): originally a word meaning *road, path, channel,* or *principle*, but in the DDJ it is the way of nature, the natural flow of the universe, the overall pattern or system that the universe wants to follow. Unlike dé which is a set of guidelines for behavior, dào is the underlying nature of the universe that can be studied and emulated. dào is nameless and formless, but its qualities are visible as it acts through the ten thousand things/creatures that make up the visible universe. Daoism, the study of dào, is the spiritual path that arose in the centuries following the writing of the DDJ around 500-580 BCE.

复 (fù), 归 (guī), 复归 (fùguī): *returning*. In the DDJ, it refers to one's return to the beginning and end of all things, starting over, returning to a zero state.

谷 (gǔ): *valley*, a low and narrow area between mountains. In the DDJ, 谷神 (gǔshén) or "spirit of the valley" is used a metaphor for the receptive, yielding nature of dào. It is a low point comparing to mountain ridges, and has no desire, no aggression, no cleverness; it is the essence of dé.

贵 (guì): literally *expensive, valuable, precious,* but in the DDJ, generally refers to a high-ranking or noble person in society.

静 (jìng): *quiet, still, motionless, tranquil.* The mind in a state of jìng is not subject to external disturbance, it is desireless and still.

君 (jūn): *sovereign, ruler, lord,* a common name for rulers of all levels in ancient China.

明 (míng): depending on context, can mean: *understand, know, comprehend, insight, make known to public, wisdom.* As with many words in Chinese, it can be used a noun (knowledge), a verb (to know), an adverb (knowingly), or an adjective (knowledgeable).

朴 (pǔ): *untreated or uncarved wood,* used in the DDJ to indicate a simple, natural state that people should return to, in harmony with Dao and without modifications or complications.

气 (qì): a key concept in Chinese philosophy and traditional Chinese medicine, it is the vital force that underlies and activates all living beings. Literally it means *gas, air* or *breath.* The energy or power of life possessed by mankind and all creatures is qì because it has gas-like characteristics. Everything in the universe is said to be the result of the movement and change of qì.

善 (shàn): *good* or *virtuous,* the social values required for good behavior and moral honesty.

身 (shēn): literally *body*, but in the DDJ it refers to a person's sense of self, something that the person feels must be defended and promoted. Attachment to shēn is often the opposite of dé.

圣人 (shèngrén): *the sage*, the most noble, virtue and sacred person, one who is an infinite existence in a finite world. Literally, "holy person." In ancient China, the holy monarch, noble scholars and religious founders were usually called sages. In the DDJ, Laozi says that the sage has no heart of his own, but is one with the hearts of the common people, fully embodying dào and living by dé.

事 (shì): *thing, matter, business, affair.* In the DDJ, it usually refers to the various phenomena and activities of nature and human society.

士 (shì): *a scholar*, the ancient Chinese literati, the lowest level of nobles in feudal society. In ancient China, shì was a scholar-official, an intellectual or member of the intellgencia. The term was used by the scholar-official to refer to themselves when addressing the Emperor. It can also refer to a military officer or commander.

天 (tiān): *sky or heaven*. More broadly, it is a symbol of dào, nature, and the universe. tiān has evolved to mean the embodiment of morality and public opinion which has formed the foundation of Chinese cultural beliefs for generations. It also is used to refer to the highest ruler, the emperor in heaven. Its counterpart is 地 (dì), earth.

天地 (tiāndì): *heaven and earth*; the world and everything that exists between sky and earth.

天下 (tiānxià): *under heaven*, everything regardless of geographic and spatial restrictions, in other words, the entire world. Historically, tiān xià was everything in the world that was divinely appointed to, and ruled by, the emperor. In the DDJ, it means the world we live in, the material world.

万物 (wànwù): *ten thousand things or creatures.* In the DDJ, all things or creatures in the universe. wàn is the largest word for a number in Chinese, so it has a secondary meaning of "the most" or "all."

为无为 (wéiwúwéi): literally, *acting without acting, doing without doing*. In the DDJ it means following nature's law, acting without attachment to the potential consequences or benefits to the one doing the action; doing as nature does, not imposing on others. By acting without acting, one is in harmony with the natural world and moves along nature's path, without disturbing the harmony and balance of nature. A ruler who practices this does not passively avoid the world, but deeply understands nature and society and acts in harmony with dào.

吾 (wú): *I, my, mine*.

无 (wú) or 无有 (wúyǒu): *not have*, the opposite of "have," the invisible, nameless, and nothingness in Dao; the source of everything.

无名 (wúmíng): *without name, nameless*. Because dào is the invisible and formless order of the universe, it is mysterious and invisible and cannot be named, yet it is the way of everything.

无事 (wúshì): *nothing happens, no interference*, just following nature by doing nothing to achieve one's goals. In the DDJ, it refers to no war, no disaster, etc.

无知 (wúzhī): *lack of knowledge or common sense*, knowing little about a subject. The DDJ advises rulers to think of themselves as wúzhī, that is, think they are not very smart, not very capable, and not very great. This humble attitude is consistent with dào.

无欲 (wúyù): *desireless*. With no personal desires or preferences, the DDJ recommends this as a way of to be followed by rulers.

心 (xīn): *heart/mind*. Traditional Chinese believed that the heart, not the brain, was the organ of thought in the human body. So, xīn can refer to the heart, the mind, or both.

阴 (yīn) **and** 阳 (yáng): In Chinese philosophy, the two complementary forces that pervade the universe, for example light/dark, large/small, growing/fading, expanding/contracting. One cannot exist without the other, for example light cannot be perceived without shadow, or cool without heat. Originally, yīn and yáng simply meant, respectively, the shady and sunny sides of a hill. Yīn represents the female; it is receptive, yielding, passive, cool, symbolized by the north side of a mountain or the south side of a body of water. yáng represents the male, it is active, bright, open, protruding, symbolized by the south side of a mountain or the north side of a body of water. In the DDJ, Laozi often recommends taking the path of yīn, and being receptive, yielding and soft.

争 (zhēng): *fight, compete.* In the DDJ, zhēng refers specifically to fighting for honor, grasping for power, and being greedy for money.

自然 (zìrán): *nature, the ongoing evolution of the universe.* Also the relationship among humanity, earth, and heaven, and between dào and nature.

Resources

We encourage you to try your hand at developing your own translation of the DDJ, or at least digging deeper into translations done by others. Here are some good online starting points:

1. Dao De Jing by Lao Zi: A Minimalist Translation by Bruce R. Linnell, PhD (2015), part of the Gutenberg Project (www.gutenberg.org/files/49965/49965-h/49965-h.htm) provides spare, almost word-for-word translations, with useful commentary.

2. The Chinese Text Project (http://ctext.org/dao-de-jing#n11636) provides very good online tools for translating the text word by word. Beware their full text translations, however, they are from Legge's 1891 translation and his attempt to make the verses rhyme in English serve only to obscure the meaning and clarity of the original.

3. The Hermetica project (http://hermetica.info) by Bradford Hatcher. He offers a minimalist, word-for-word translation of the DDJ, and his "matrix translation" is an interesting resource for seeing alternate meanings of each word in the DDJ.

4. The Dao Bums (www.thedaobums.com) is a wonderful online discussion forum for serious students of the DDJ, and includes chapter-by-chapter discussions of the finer points of the text.

5. The Wiktionary (https://en.wiktionary.org/wiki), part of the Wikipedia family of websites, is a useful tool for digging deeper into the meanings of individual Chinese characters.

6. Lao Tzu's Tao Te Ching Translators' Resource (www.taoteching.co.uk) by Arthur W. Hummel, offers a variety of free translators' tools.

7. Google Translate (https://translate.google.com) can be useful, but it gives modern translations which can be quite different from the meanings that the words had 2500 years ago.

About The Authors

Jeff Pepper (author) is President and CEO of Imagin8 Press, and has written dozens of books about Chinese language and culture. Over his thirty-five year career he has founded and led several successful computer software firms, including one that became a publicly traded company. He's authored two software related books and was awarded three U.S. software patents.

Dr. Xiao Hui Wang (translator), has an M.S. in Information Science, an M.D. in Medicine, a Ph.D. in Neurobiology and Neuroscience, and 25 years experience in academic and clinical research. She has taught Chinese for over 10 years and has extensive experience in translating Chinese to English and English to Chinese.

Made in the USA
Monee, IL
15 June 2021

d0c433fa-e948-465d-bf71-deb4d14be0b4R01